THE
SHAREHOLDER

This book is dedicated to the erstwhile partners of Buckmaster & Moore, James Capel, Carr Sebag, Cazenove, Foster & Braithwaite, Gilbert Eliott, Greenwell, Grenfell & Colegrave, Grieveson Grant, Hedderwick Stirling Grumbar, Henderson Crosthwaite, Hoare Govett, J M Finn, Keith Bayley Rogers, Kitkat & Aitken, Laurence Prust, McAnally Montgomery, Messels, Montagu Loebl Stanley, Mullens, Northcote, Panmure Gordon, Quilter Goodison, Raphael Zorn, Rowe & Pitman, Scott Goff Hancock, Scrimgeour Kemp-Gee, Sheppards & Chase, Strauss Turnbull, Williams de Broe Hill Chaplin, and Wood Mackenzie who decided, back in 1980, that whatever else I was destined to be, it was certainly not a stockbroker.

THE
SHAREHOLDER

The Truth About Wider Share Ownership

SIMON ROSE

MERCURY BOOKS
Published by W.H. Allen & Co. Plc

First published in 1989 by Mercury Books
Published in paperback 1991
by Mercury Books
Gold Arrow Publications Ltd
862 Garratt Lane, London SW17 0NB

Cartoons by Ken Pyne

Set in Palatino by Phoenix Photosetting
Printed and bound in Great Britain by
Mackays of Chatham PLC, Chatham, Kent

British Library Cataloguing in Publication Data

Rose, Simon
    The shareholder: the truth about wider
        share ownership
    1 Great Britain. Stockmarkets;—for
        private investment
    I.1 Title
    332.64'241
    ISBN 1–85252–036–1

FOREWORD
BY THE CHAIRMAN OF
THE LONDON STOCK EXCHANGE

Shares are risk investments and can go down as well as up. That is the first thing anyone should know about shares. Investors should therefore always keep a sense of perspective and a sense of humour. The sense of humour is needed to cope with the inevitable, but we hope only occasional, bad decisions.

On the other hand, and this is where the sense of perspective comes in, share investment can be extremely rewarding and certainly more interesting than the bank or building society.

Simon Rose's own very sharp sense of humour is well displayed in all his writing and broadcasting and this book is no exception. It berates everybody involved in the market without exception and any investor looking for favourable mention of anyone involved with investment should return the book to the shelves right now. Do not think that you, the private investor, will escape scot free either: you too will need a sense of humour and perhaps a few pills to keep your blood pressure under control.

Within the barrage of criticism, there are plenty of home truths. Simon Rose works on the reverse of the sugar-coated pill theory: he coats his pearls of wisdom with a sometimes unsavoury cover.

Nonetheless, his book is an excellent read for the private investor: his sense of humour is clear; his sense of perspective? Well, judge for yourself.

Andrew Hugh Smith

INTRODUCTION

I am a keen advocate of wider share ownership. Once upon a time, not so very long ago, such a declaration would have led to much turning-up of noses in certain quarters. In this new era of People's Capitalism, though, I am practically trampled underfoot by worthy souls protesting that spreading the ownership of shares more widely is a jolly good thing; government ministers, Bank of England officials, the Stock Exchange, industrialists, stockbrokers, even members of the Labour Party.

But in addition to being a keen advocate of wider share ownership, I am a somewhat disillusioned advocate of wider share ownership. We don't really have 'People's Capitalism' yet in Britain. We don't have anything near it. What we have instead is a great many people owning one or two shares which they bought by filling in a form in a newspaper. They did so, by and large, not through any desire to support British industry or to invest for the future, but for the simple reason that absolutely everyone was saying it was the easiest way to make a few bob with very little effort. Most of them wouldn't recognise a stockbroker if one bit them on the nose. They know nothing about investment and understand very little indeed about the world of stocks and shares.

In the introduction to the second edition of *Fair Shares – A Layman's Guide to Buying and Selling Stocks and Shares* which was published by Mercury before the Crash of October 1987, I wrote 'Investing in the stock market without the slightest notion of what you are buying is nothing less than a gamble, pure and simple. It is not investment. It is fortunate for the newcomers that the privatisation programme has coincided with a long period of rising stock market prices. Yet shares do not go on climbing forever. When the stock market turns savagely downwards, as it surely is going to do at some stage, many investors new to the stock market, who have perhaps over-reached themselves, won't have the slightest idea of what has hit them.' How many of those newcomers to the stock market, or even some of the old-timers, had prepared themselves psychologically for the spectacular fireworks show put on by the stock markets of the world in October 1987?

In the wake of the Crash and mini-Crash, all those people who had earlier been shouting about wider share ownership suddenly went all quiet. We hardly heard a peep from them for months afterwards. After encouraging the public to invest their savings in privatisation issues, it was almost as if the preachers of People's Capitalism were trying to pretend the whole thing had never happened.

The reason for my disillusionment is that the Government and the Stock Exchange do not seem to have come up with any way of deepening share ownership other than through the sale of state businesses, which is pretty much the same as standing on street corners offering £5 notes for only £4 each. At the time of writing, the Chancellor Norman Lamont has called for institutions to come up with some bright ideas for bringing share dealing to the high street and perhaps something will come of this.

> The claims of Government ministers that we are now a nation of shareholders appeared a little shaky when four budding Brains of Britain were asked by chairman Robert Robinson: 'What is the usual length of the Stock Exchange Account?'
>
> The answer came back, quick as a flash: 'Two years.'
>
> The other contestants then had a shot at it: 'Six weeks', 'twenty-one days', and 'six months' were their responses.

Something has to happen if the idea of wider share ownership is not to evaporate completely. Despite the number of shareholders having risen from two million to eleven million since 1979, the number of active, experienced investors has remained exactly the same. There were around 300,000 private investors a decade ago with a portfolio of ten shares or more. That number has not budged since. The influence of the private investor on the affairs of the stock market continues to decline, as that of the institutions grows ever larger.

Many stockbrokers have washed their hands of so-called 'small' investors altogether. The Stock Exchange continues to move the goalposts all over the field, making investment as convenient for the institutional investor as possible but uprooting them again whenever private investors seem about to score a goal. 'Lawson the Tax Reformer' and his successors in fact have ended up doing very little to diminish the tax advantages enjoyed by the institutions, and the pension funds in particular. Why should people invest for the future directly, handling their own investments, when they could do so through a tax-exempt pension fund?

Still, why not look on the bright side? I suppose I

should be thankful that in Britain it isn't actually *illegal* for individuals to buy and sell shares!

In *Fair Shares*, I explained the theory of stock market investment. The practice, however, is often very different. In some quarters the treatment of private investors is nothing short of scandalous, as is the way our interests as a group are constantly being over-ridden and ignored, simply because we cannot speak with one voice, as the institutions can. The position of the private investor is still a precarious and lonely one.

I don't see any reason why I should have to be fair and even-handed here. It's my book. I intend being as opinionated as I can, and why not? If I believe in my own mind that the gentlemen of the Treasury know as much about investment as I know about soufflé-making, that stockbrokers are rapacious financial muggers with no morals or scruples whatsoever, that all institutional fund managers are in reality horned servants of the devil, that the members of the Council of the Stock Exchange are really Soviet agents and that all private investors are wonderful, intelligent, sophisticated individuals who deserve knighthoods for their perseverence in the face of such overwhelming odds, why should I not be allowed to say so?

Even if you don't agree with all my ideas, I hope you will have a lot of fun along the way.

The earlier edition of this book was written in the wake of the Crash of 1987. Although I have updated most of the information in this edition, I have kept some of the examples from 1987 where they are pertinent. Investors should not forget just how unforgiving and ferocious the stock market can be at its worst and should remember some of the idiocies that led up to it. There is no reason to think another crash is impossible in the future.

Simon Rose

CONTENTS

1

The Cautious Investor

This book is aimed not so much at those punters who love dabbling in the stock market, wheeling and dealing, buying and selling within the Stock Exchange Account and stagging every new issue. It is intended more for the sedate investor, the person who is content to build up his or her portfolio over a number of years, the person who is that most virtuous of people, the long-term investor.

It is possible, I suppose, for someone who is incredibly talented at stock market investment to punt around on a daily basis, making a killing each time almost without fail. I know of no-one who can do this successfully who isn't terribly well-connected within the City and thus able to pick up the sort of juicy gossip that is denied to most of us, but perhaps such paragons do exist somewhere. I know a great number of people who *believe* that they are investment wizards, refusing to believe the evidence to the contrary presented by their bank balances. Whenever they add up the numbers, they always seem able to claim that it is only one or two investments turning a little sour that has prevented them from being as rich as Croesus himself.

The people who really do become wealthy from punting like this, of course, are the stockbrokers and banks. It is still relatively rare for stockbrockers to charge fees for any of their services. They exist instead on the commission charged on each transaction and, as far as they are concerned, the more often their clients deal, the happier they are. The real punters can always be sure of a great welcome from their stockbrokers. After all, it is they who are helping to pay for the Porsches and the BMWs, the grand houses in the stockbroker belt and the wonderful lunches that force the loosening of the stockbrokers' belts.

> Just in its fifth and final year,
> His University Career
> Was blasted by the new and dread
> Necessity of earning bread.
> He was compelled to join a firm
> Of Brokers – in the summer term!
>
> And even now, at twenty-five,
> He has to WORK to keep alive!
> Yes! All day long from 10 till 4!
> For half the year or even more;
> With but an hour or two to spend
> At luncheon with a city friend.
>
> (*from Belloc's Cautionary Verses*)

Yet it may be the more cautious investor who is the more successful over the long run. One of the most compelling arguments in favour of stock market investment, as opposed to 'safer' havens such as the building society, is its extraordinary performance over the long term. £1,000 left

in the building society to accumulate interest at the end of 1945 would, by the close of play in 1990, have been worth £8,990 to a basic-rate taxpayer. That same investment, with net income reinvested, made in an average portfolio of shares would have grown to £108,820, according to figures from Barclays de Zoete Wedd! The figure to a non-taxpayer would be £243,830. Those are pretty impressive numbers and I have used them on many occasions to illustrate the wonders of the market.

Yet income is crucial to those computations. BZW's index of shares suggests that by excluding income from the equation, the portfolio of shares would have risen to just £26,870. With inflation taken into account, that looks pretty unimpressive and certainly nothing to break open the bubbly about.

Income is terribly important, and that is something the punters amongst us frequently forget, believing that those who talk about the value of dividends are incredibly fuddy-duddy and not worth passing the time of day with. Immediately after the 1987 Crash, income was king again, but only for a few weeks. Yet income is real. Share prices aren't. Shares are only worth what you can sell them for and, until you have actually disposed of them and are holding the cheque in your grubby hand, the price in the newspaper is just a number, nothing more.

Dividends are real money. Once a company has paid it to you, it can't ask for it back, even if it needs it.

A letter to the *Times* aggrievedly claimed that: 'Sexism is clearly alive and well in the City. What other explanation can there possibly be for the fact that, although our holdings in Rolls-Royce are identical, my husband received a dividend of £2.63, whereas I received a mere £2.62?'

The punters point to the lamentably low average yield on shares and ask why anybody not addicted to the fascination of watching paint drying should get excited about dividends. It is true that most shares have a low yield. At the time of writing, the market as a whole yields a bare 4.6% and, even at the start of the eighties, when inflation was roaring away, the average figure only just managed to touch 7%. The average yield over the long-term is something around 5.25%. Yet it is not the current yield on shares that is important, but the yield in years to come.

A company that prospers ought to increase its dividend payout to shareholders. The table shows the growth in each year of the past decade for the companies that comprise the All-Share Index.

year	80	81	82	83	84	85	86	87	88	89
% increase	3	9	6	14	16	12	14	18	18	16

SOURCE: PHILLIPS & DREW

But the shareholder will only appreciate the true effect of this if he holds onto his shares. Marks and Spencer, for instance, have a yield just two-thirds of that of the average share at the time I am writing these words. With the shares at 257p the yield is 3.3% gross, or 2.5% to the basic-rate taxpayer. It doesn't sound too scintillating.

Back in 1978 the shares could be bought at 35p, when the yield was just 3% to the basic-rate taxpayer. One could be forgiven for thinking that nothing ever changes. Yet the dividend has risen steadily over the years. Someone who bought the shares then and still held them would have received a dividend of 6.4p net for 1990. Whereas, for a new investor paying 257p, that would be a yield of 2.5% net, for the person who has paid just 35p for the shares, the yield is

[17]

a whopping 18.3% net or 24.4% when expressed as a gross figure. And, because the dividend has increased steadily over the years, the shares have risen to seven times their original value. Had this not happened, the current yield would of course be completely out of line with other shares on the stock market.

Net yield	80	81	82	83	84	85	86	87	88	89	90
Build Soc.	10.5	9.1	8.5	6.8	7.0	7.6	6.0	5.3	4.4	6.1	7.0
M&S		4.9	5.4	6.6	7.4	8.9	9.7	11.1	12.9	14.6	16.0	18.3

Although the punter may have been able to benefit from some of the rise in the price of the shares, by moving in and out of this, or any other stock, he will not benefit from the steadily rising yield. He will instead be buying at the current yield all the time. There will obviously be times when dividends will not be increased but, unless British industry

Searching for an unusual Christmas present, a stockbroker went into a pet shop in the Square Mile. Homing in on the parrots, he was shown one that cost £500.

'Good grief!' he exclaimed. 'That seems a bit steep.'

'Ah,' said the shopkeeper. 'But it does speak fluent French and has O-level Maths. This one,' he continued, 'costs £1,000. It speaks Italian like a native and has a PhD in Economics.'

'Well, how much is that one?' asked the broker, indicating a rather scraggy looking bird.

'Ah, that one costs £2,000.'

'What on earth does it do?'

'It doesn't appear to do anything at all, but the other two call it the Senior Partner.'

gets its collective knickers well and truly caught in the mangle, this is more likely to be a temporary hiccough than anything else.

There is another excellent reason why those who buy good investments and stick with them will do better than the dabblers. It is one that is all to easy to forget. *It costs money to buy and sell shares.* A stockbroker is these days likely to charge you at least £20 for even the smallest deal, with around 1.5% or more levied on more substantial ones. The more often you wheel and deal, the more delighted is your broker and the friendlier he is likely to be towards you. Why should he work for a living when he has clients like you?

There is not only the commission to be taken into consideration, of course, but the spread as well. On average, this will be around 5% between the buying and selling price of a share. Deal regularly and these 5%'s, together with the commissions, will cut savagely into your investment performance.

In the first series of independent television's The Stocks and Shares Show, a nominal commission charge did little to dampen down the contestants' enthusiasm for chopping and changing their portfolios every week. Given a notional £10,000 to invest, they each tended to sell three shares worth a total value of £7,500 each week, reinvesting the proceeds in three new shares. Taking into account 5% spreads and real commission rates instead of the £60 charged by the game organisers, they would have faced a penalty of about £600 each week. Over the 12-week run of the show, each contestant would have found £7,200 of their precious capital eaten up. This is not really a criticism of the show's producers, who obviously could not make the game unduly realistic without making it unbelievably tedious at the same time. Yet it would have been interesting to see

[19]

how keen the four amateur dabblers would have been to churn their portfolios if they had been dealing with the real costs of real stockbrokers and market-makers.

It is a terribly hard lesson to learn, but if you believe you have found a share which is good value, stick with it for as long as you believe that it is still good value. Don't suddenly get excited because the price of the share has risen sharply unless you believe it to be seriously over-valued. It is easy to say that, of course. I wish it was as easy to do in practice. There are times when I come close to tears, opening the inside back page of the *Financial Times* in the morning and seeing the sickeningly healthy prices and dividends of some of the shares that I have foolishly allowed myself to sell, simply because I had a good profit.

2

Whither Share Ownership, or should that be wither?

Let's not beat about the bush. The whole idea of wider share ownership was an accident, pure and simple. In late 1984, when the Government was getting ready to sell off British Telecom, all the indications were that the institutions were not particularly interested. I can still recall jokes doing the rounds of the City along the lines of: 'The first prize is 10,000 shares in British Telecom. The second prize is 20,000 shares in British Telecom' – followed by collapse of stout fund managers bowled over by their own amazing wit and one port too many.

It was well-known at the time that you could not hope to sell even a moderately large company without the goodwill of the City's fund managers, let alone one as large as BT, the biggest sale to date on the stock market.

The answer, as we now know of course, was to angle it instead towards us, the public. Some chap at the Treasury probably came in by bus one day and, glancing at an ad for washing powder or something, had a brainwave. If Mr & Mrs Public will buy soap when you advertise it enough, perhaps they will buy shares too? I don't know who it was who came up with this original thought but no doubt if we go back over the lists of knighthoods in the past few years, his name will be there somewhere.

In private, stockbrockers are wont to cast aspersions upon the intelligence of the fund managers who are their clients. Fund managers, for their part, are usually less than complimentary about stockbrokers, frequently informing them of the fact even to their face.

Over lunch one day, one fund manager was regaling me with tales of how useless all the stockbrokers he knew were and then said: 'Actually, that's a bit unfair. One did give me some very valuable advice only this morning. I couldn't for the life of me remember if this restaurant was in Finsbury Circus or Finsbury Square. So I rang one of the stockbrokers who has been pestering me for business for some time. He told me straightaway and, what's more, he got it right.'

Fund managers are the closest thing the human race has to sheep. Point one important looking one in a direction and the others will rush after him. He could decide he was really a lemming and jump over a cliff and, if the fall didn't kill him, he would soon be squashed flat by a torrent of fund managers landing on his head. These creatures almost all eschew original thought. Think for yourself and you stand a chance of committing the cardinal sin, that of being wrong. They all crave instead to be as average as possible. The nearer to the average performance of the stock market they get, the happier they seem to be.

With the enthusiasm of the public building up for British Telecom, the combined brain power of the institutional fund managers began to wonder if there might not be

Whither Share Ownership, or should that be wither?

something in it. They soon realised that they wouldn't be able to buy enough shares to give themselves an average stock market weighting in the shares and that tipped the balance. In order to have the right proportion of the shares in their portfolio they would have to apply for more than they needed or else buy them once trading had begun. Nothing more was needed to make the issue a success than the awakening of this general perception in the City, which only took root a few weeks before the shares were launched on the market.

The rest, as they say, is history.

However, it seems that somebody at the Treasury forgot the real reason for BT's success and so we had the un-edifying spectacle of privatisation issue after privatisation issue being sold through heavy public advertising and kind-ly, if not outrightly generous, pricing of the shares. There was no attempt to run an education programme at the same time to explain what the stock market was really about, bar the inclusion of a booklet that would have insulted the intelligence of a two-year-old child. I remain unconvinced that its contents are even now well understood at the Treasury, however!

So the majority of new 'investors' were left, after one or two of these issues, with the impression that all you need to do to make money on the stock market is fill in a form and send off your cheque. As easy as falling off a log, except that you don't get as wet. So we had the ludicrous situation, when share fever was at its height, of companies like Tie Rack and Sock Shop having their issues 83 and 53 times oversubscribed respectively! Yet look how they fared.

Several surveys have shown that only a minority of these new shareholders have a good idea of how to sell their shares and a substantial number don't even realise that you *can* sell them. Particularly in the wake of the collapse of the stock market in October 1987, many will have been left with the impression that shares are profitable only in their early days on the stock market, when they soar to a premium, but become riskier the longer you leave them untouched. Time after time, small investors have sold new issues heavily, thanking their lucky stars that they have managed to get their money back out of the vicious jaws of the stock market, and deposited it again with those nice people at the building society.

Something like four-fifths of all investors in Britain have bought their shares through a new issue and there seems little reason to believe that many will progress to the next stage, investing in shares that are already traded on the stock market and beginning to build up a diversified port-folio. There is nothing wrong with having just one or two shares, provided that you realise the great inherent risk of having all your eggs in just one or two baskets, sub-stantially-built though those baskets may be.

There seems to be a realisation within the Treasury that, unless a completely different approach is adopted, the only way the new wave of investors can be persuaded to increase the number of shares they own is by keeping the number of large new issues flowing. This was made abun-dantly clear by Nigel Lawson in an interview with the *Financial Times* at the beginning of 1987: 'What we have demonstrated is that if you have a company with some-thing of a household name and suitable for small investors, then do a certain amount of advertising and you can get a huge increase in the number of shareholders.' Perhaps the way he said it at the time wasn't quite as cynical as it appears in print. Perhaps it was.

The then Chancellor said that the Stock Exchange should relax its rules so that existing quoted companies could raise capital from new shareholders, to all intents and purposes like a second or third tranche of a privatisation issue. Apart from conveniently trying to pass the Wider Share Ownership baton to the Stock Exchange before it exploded in his hand, the chancellor seemed to forget that not only Stock Exchange rules, but also the law of the land, insist that existing shareholders get first crack of a substantial issue of new shares. These pre-emption rights are an integral part of the rules attempting to ensure that all shareholders are treated equally. If a company could issue extra shares without offering them first to existing shareholders, the proportion of equity held by those investors would diminish, as would their influence on the company's affairs.

Even without the doctrine of pre-emption to stand in the way of this idea, one can hardly imagine many companies willing to go to the expense of a privatisation-style issue just to drag in loads of extra small investors. In the minds of the majority of directors, private investors are a pain in the neck, if not a pain in another more sensitve part of the anatomy, taking up a great deal of time and expense to service.

It would probably also be illegal for private companies to advertise their shares in the manner which the Government has been able to get away with. 'Be Part of It' or 'The Big One' may be construed as inducements to buy shares and such inducements are positively illegal. In the new era of the Financial Services Act, when it can be a crime for a company to sneeze without having the permission of a raft of financial advisers, it is highly unlikely that posters declaring 'Hurrah for Hanson,' or 'Go for GEC' would be allowed to see the light of day.

Indeed, since broaching the idea, not another dicky-bird has been heard about it from either Lawson's successors or the Treasury, a sure sign it has been forgotten and that the

Anatoly Bogaty defected from the KGB in 1982, seeking asylum in the United States. In 1987, he expressed a wish to return to Moscow. His reason? Not intellectual dissatisfaction with the West. No, Bogaty and his wife had invested heavily in the market and were wiped out on Black Monday.

policy-makers have gone back to their earlier plans of selling state industry after state industry to the public until they run out of companies, at which point we will presumably be told that we finally have 'People's Capitalism' in Britain.

The 1987 Budget was generally held to be a wonderful one for the rich and for the moderately well-off. For the private investor, however, it was a mixed blessing. It was odd indeed that at the very time when the Government was most concerned to spread share ownership as widely as possible, it should penalise the gains made on share transactions even more heavily. Until then, net gains of up to £6,600 in any one financial year were free of tax. The tax, if applicable, was levied at the flat rate of 30%.

Now Capital Gains Tax is levied at the investor's marginal Income Tax rate which may be 25 or 40%. More importantly, however, the level at which CGT bites has been reduced to £5,500. This, presumably, will bring a far greater number of people within the net of the tax at a time when personal wealth is increasing. This would not be so bad perhaps were Capital Gains Tax not such a pig's breakfast of a tax and about as easy to comprehend as a poorly translated manual for a Japanese hi-fi.

Every CGT-paying investor I meet grumbles about the indexation of the tax and the onerous obligations it makes upon the individual (or his accountant). In the light of this widespread discontent, I had been at a loss to understand just why the Government were so unwilling to simplify the whole thing until someone pointed me in the direction of that wonderful volume of bedside reading, 'Inland Revenue Statistics 1990'. It records that in 1987–8, the latest period for which there are accurate statistics apparently, just 120,000 people paid CGT. Although this seems, to all the stockbrokers I have pointed it out to, surprisingly low, presumably the Inland Revenue does know how many are paying the tax. It explains why the Treasury aren't too bothered by the troubles it causes. It is interesting to see how the number of people paying CGT has fallen over the years. At the end of the 1960s, there were around 400,000. By the beginning of the 1980s, there were just 200,000. That evidence hardly squares with the idea that share ownership has been spreading widely throughout the land. The number could soon be set to rise quite sharply however, now that capital gains and income have been equalised in their tax treatment, bar the CGT exemption of course.

Although the Conservatives have acquired a reputation as tax reformers, they have done nothing yet to tackle the extraordinary tax privileges of the pension funds. Individuals are given tax relief on money invested in pension funds and employers are able to set the contributions off against their own tax bills. Within the fund itself, the money is free from all taxes, incurring no Capital Gains Tax and no Income Tax. At retirement, a substantial portion of this cash is available as a tax-free sum. Cast your mind back to the BZW figures showing how well an investor has done over the years who has not been liable to pay any tax and you will begin to realise the truly magnificent extent of the Government's generosity. In a Centre for Policy Studies' paper on the privileges enjoyed by pension funds, Philip Chappell calculates that about £25,000 million a year is being sheltered from Income Tax with about another £15,000 million a year safe from Capital Gains Tax. Treating pension funds just as other mortals would enable a Chancellor to take a substantial axe to Income Tax rates. As Chappell says: 'Those who champion wider ownership regret that the form of saving particularly favoured by fiscal privilege enforces institutional ownership and denies to the individual the right to spend his money as he chooses. How patronising that an employer distributes 90% of remuneration to be spent as the employee chooses, but insists on retaining the last 10% to be saved for old age under a sheltered tax umbrella! A free market should facilitate access to savings, rather than insist they be kept for retirement: a good tax system gives everybody the extra wherewithal with which to save, allowing different decisions according to changing needs.'

Hear, hear. To a large extent because of the bias in savings caused by the pension funds' tax privileges, the influence of private investors on the stock market as a whole, and on the companies quoted there, continues to decrease. Back in 1957, two-thirds of all shares were owned by indi-

---

Lonnie F Patterson of Urbana, Illinois may be regretting his decision to invest the proceeds of an armed robbery in a savings account, sensible though the desire to earn interest on his ill-gotten gains was.

What was not particularly sensible was choosing Urbana's First Federal of Champaign Savings & Loan as a home for his money. For not only had he robbed that particular S&L just three days earlier, but the teller at the window was the very same one who had on that occasion handed the cash to him at the point of his gun.

Not surprisingly, Patterson was arrested.

---

viduals in Britain. The institutions had a bare 18%. Now the positions have been entirely reversed, with private investors owning less than a fifth of all UK shares and the institutions over two-thirds. In many of the top 100 British companies, individuals own nearer to 10% of the shares and, despite the increasing interest in the stock market over the past few years, that number has declined steadily since the Conservatives came to power.

25% of Lloyds Bank's shares were owned by individuals in 1982, according to its Annual Report; by 1987, the proportion was 20.9%; by 1990 just 18%. In 1982, 34.5% of Burmah shares were in private hands; by 1986, the figure was 21.7%; by 1990 only 15.7%. The 1961 figure for Coats Patons was a massive 64.4%; by 1986 19.1% of Coats Viyella shares were held by individuals; by 1989 just 17.0%. 26.7% of Barclays shares were owned by private investors as recently as 1984; by 1987 they accounted for 18.4%; by 1990 a mere 15.1%. Such is the mirage of wider share ownership, visible to Government ministers and the worthies at the Stock Exchange, and invisible to everybody out there in the real world.

It can't even be claimed with any great justification that the privatisation programme has met the aims set for it by ministers. The original intention was to foster competition. That was then submerged by the government's enthusiasm to let the public in on each subsequent issue. There is little benefit to competition to be had by floating companies into the private sector in exactly the same form in which they operated in the public sector. A study in mid-1987 by economists at Newcastle University found that British Telecom's efficiency was no better than before privatisation, concluding that smaller phone companies around the world are more efficient than their larger brethren.

Having persuaded ten million or so people to buy

[30]

Moves by various communist governments abroad to set up
elementary stock exchanges may not be as far away from Marx-
ist theory as many might suppose. In Leslie Page's study of the
father of communism, *Karl Marx and the Critical Examination of
His Works*, there is a letter dated June 1986 from Karl to his
uncle, Lion Philips.

He was the founder of the electrical giant of the same name. In
the letter Karl admits to having speculated on the stock market. 'I
won more than £400 and will, when the entanglement of political
conditions offers new scope, begin anew.'

shares in these issues, it is by no means apparent that the
public's earlier antipathetic attitude towards business and
the stock market has changed markedly. A poll published
in June 1988 found that six out of ten people opposed plans
to privatise the water and electricity industries and found a
majority of people favouring a 'mainly socialist society.'
Even allowing for the fact that, using polls, you can probably find a majority of Britons who believe that the sun
revolves around the earth, this seems a depressingly
familiar response and hardly encourages one to believe that
there has been a sea-change in sentiment towards the stock
market or the public sector.

Some ministers have pointed with pride to the increasing
number of companies where workers own part of the business through shares. I have seen a couple of studies purporting to show that companies which give employees a
share of the profits in such a way do better than those who
stick with the 'them' and 'us' attitude. The latest research,
undertaken at the University of Wales Institute of Science
and Technology, found that although the overwhelming
majority of workers liked to own shares in the companies
for which they worked, they did not become more 'profit

conscious' as a result, nor did they feel that they benefited directly as a consequence of an increase in profitability. The research claimed that job satisfaction, job security, profitability and communications with management were rarely affected by the distribution of shares among the workforce.

To some extent, this would seem to be backed up by the industrial unrest at VSEL in Barrow-in-Furness in 1988. Privatised in 1986, around a quarter of the company is owned by its employees. Four-fifths of them took up the offer to buy shares when it was floated off from British Shipbuilders. Industrial relations have been less than rosy, however, and in the midst of a dispute over when holidays could be taken, union leader Frank Ward said 'Nobody gives a bugger about the shares. They never saw buying them as anything other than a transaction which would help them to put down a deposit on a house or buy a bathroom.'

On the other hand the National Freight Consortium was bought out by its employees and management in 1982 and has given the impression of being one big happy family, with van drivers touting for custom for the firm as they go about their business. Perhaps that has something to do with a 64-fold increase in the value of the shares by the beginning of 1991. A founder subscriber at that stage would have been getting a gross annual yield on his or her original investment of some 224%!

Perhaps I have been painting an unduly pessimistic picture. I have no wish to make investors run for the nearest bunker to take shelter until the investment climate improves sufficiently to warrant emerging once more. I only want to point out that so much of the spouting off about wider share ownership and People's Capitalism and the like is just so much guff. It is going to take decades, rather than years, to change the attitudes of the great

British public towards shares and the stock market. The ludicrous Financial Services Act which is mind-bogglingly complex, has probably taken us several steps backwards. Its voluminous rules and regulations are enough to frighten off even the most experienced investor. The mattress as a haven for savings may seem a far more attractive proposition to some people, particularly as you do not yet need to fill in umpteen complicated forms to stash your cash there.

There is one favourable wind blowing in the right direction which may help the advancement of the cause. That is the so-called Inheritance Effect. Two-thirds of us now own our own homes. It has been some time since people selling their homes expected to get a lower price than when they bought it. Instead, property is considered to be a cast-iron, fool-proof investment, with the added advantage that you can live in it as well. Even painting a house in vile colours, installing awful double-glazed windows, concreting over the back garden and other such aberrations cannot, it seems, dent the property spiral. And while prices may not continue climbing forever, a great many people are already inhabiting some handsome profits.

What happens when a house-owning couple die? If their children already have a house, it is unlikely that they will want to own another one. Instead, unless they have children of their own who want to get their tootsies on the housing ladder, they will turn the property into cash and invest it. There is only so much life assurance that can be bought (most of it benefiting the life companies as much as those buying the policies). So much of it will flow into the stock market as direct investment, some through unit trusts and investment trusts and some as direct purchases of stocks and shares.

A total of 50% of pensioner households own their own homes and the merchant bank Morgan Grenfell has calculated that half of the middle-aged households in this country will inherit property typically worth £35,000. By the end of the century, property worth nearly £9,000 million a year will be handed on in every year, an inheritance worth as much as the Government got from privatising British Gas and British Telecom together.

If all that money sloshing around doesn't turn us into a share-owning democracy, then nothing will.

3

Wanted: Stockbroker willing to look after small private clients

It is always nice to hear from your friendly stockbroker. The clients of one London firm received a letter early in 1988 that began thus:

'We are writing to inform you that after Tuesday, 31st March, 1988 we will no longer be able to continue to provide our private client service to you. The decision to withdraw this service has been made after careful consideration. After March 31st we will no longer be in a position to execute orders on your behalf.

. . . 'We would like to take this opportunity to thank you for your valued custom over the years.'

By accident the letter was sent to a good many of the firm's institutional clients as well, causing some hilarity at those establishments. For private investors, however, such letters have of late become all too common. The explanation is simple. It costs each stockbroking firm a certain amount to process each bargain. The procedure involved in settling a Stock Exchange transaction and ensuring that the new

The Somerset-based stockbroking firm of Godfray Derby, part of the National Investment Group, has its own form of health warning for investors – its address. To find its offices in Wells you go to The Market Place and then look out for Penniless Porch!

investor's name goes onto the company's share register is still a very involved one, with pieces of paper flying to and fro in a manner that would have sent Dickens or Kafka scurrying for their pens. The big City firms are having to pay rents far higher than in the provinces while their staff get salaries that sound more like premium bond prizes than remuneration for employment.

London firms estimate that it costs them between £30 and £50 to process each deal. Before Big Bang, when commissions were fixed, the institutions (or so we are told) apparently subsidised private investors. Private clients are now, for many firms, simply too fiddly to bother with without that subsidy. Although in 1987 we transacted three-quarters of all deals struck in UK shares, the value of those shares, however, was only just a fifth of the total figure. That isn't too surprising. We small investors are, by our very nature, small.

As if that were not enough to be going on with, private client brokers have been hit heavily by the onerous requirements of the Financial Services Act, the best intentioned and most ill-executed piece of legislation one could possibly imagine. There are many drawbacks to the Act from the investor's point of view, one of the most visible being that every single client seeking advice from a stockbroker must have signed a Client Agreement Letter before being permitted to deal. Some firms have had to send out tens of thousands of these voluminous documents. One leading private client broker's letter ran to 20 pages, with 32 clauses and 5 appendices. The firm apologised for the fact that this 'might give clients a nosebleed' and felt it sensible to run a prize draw to encourage replies, with entry restricted to those who returned their forms. As another broker pointed out in a letter to his clients: 'These rules are detailed and, frankly, are more time consuming and costly to administer than is needed for the protection of clients of Members of the Stock Exchange.'

The following letter was sent out by one stockbroker to its clients:

'This is an advance warning that, as part of the provisions of the Financial Services Act, we will shortly be sending all of you rather complicated letters for you to sign and return.

'These define the nature of the service we provide and are designed to ensure that no client is in any doubt about what this is. They will also demonstrate that we have on file all relevant information about you, to ensure that we are not unwittingly providing a service inappropriate to your circumstances.

'It is an intensely bureaucratic exercise and we apologise in advance for any inconvenience or brain damage which it may cause, but we have no choice.'

It is hardly surprising that some well-established clients of brokers have made a fuss about the detailed questions being asked on employment, income, tax status and the like. Yet the new rules insist that brokers 'know your client.' If a client sets dealing parameters which are then ignored by a broker, he risks the possibility of legal action. It is this possible threat which has made the Client Agreement Letters, as with so much else connected with the

Financial Services Act, so hideously convoluted and complicated. If a client sets himself dull and safe dealing parameters and then decides he want to take a 'flyer' on something, the broker may refuse to carry out the order. Should the investment go wrong, a litigious-minded client could always claim that it was the wrong sort of thing for the broker to have put him into. The majority of private client stockbroking firms do not record all their conversations, unlike the institutional ones, so it would merely be one person's word against another's.

Clients also have to say whether they would be willing to receive unsolicited phone calls or not. Most stockbrokers need to be able to contact discretionary clients in the event, perhaps, of a takeover bid or a surge in the price of one of the client's shares. It obviously does not make sense if a broker cannot ring his client to discuss a particular investment opportunity, particularly as such calls would only rarely be made and might signal the need for a client to act very quickly. Yet, on the other hand, as the form says; 'Although the ability to telephone you in this way is likely to increase the effectiveness of our services to you, you will forgo certain statutory rights that you might otherwise have entitling you to undo an investment transaction which you enter into as a result of an uninvited call.' In other words, by doing the sensible thing and permitting unsolicited calls, your rights are actually reduced. Why brokers should be restricted in this way, when insurance and unit trust groups are allowed to cold-call whoever they like, is totally beyond me.

You can also put restrictions on the type of investments in which to invest, excluding tobacco or armaments from your portfolio for instance or even, should you so wish, any whose chairmen were born under the sign of Leo or who have an 'R' in their name. Some wags have suggested returning the forms with a request only to invest in firms involved with sex, drugs, rock and roll. However, it is likely that any humour to be drawn from Client Agreement Letters will probably be lost on the stockbrokers who have had to send out, get back and put onto computer hundreds of thousands of the things.

Although much of what is contained within Client Agreement Letters is laid down by the rules of the various regulatory bodies such as The Securities Association it is clear that, because of investors' ability under Section 62 of the Act to take legal action against firms which breach the rules, some of these letters are designed more to protect the broker than the client.

It isn't only stockbrokers who send out Client Agreement Letters, of course, but every single investment adviser. So you can't escape simply by popping into your local financial intermediary. One parent complained indignantly to a national newspaper that he had to fill in a form when he opened a savings account for his five-year-old daughter!

Despite the effects of the Financial Services Act and the withdrawal of some of the large City-based stockbroking firms from the private client market, someone looking for a broker could still find himself spoilt for choice. For, despite our habit of doing lots of deals worth only a little money, private clients do generate a great deal of commission. One of the results of Big Bang is that the big institutions pay their stockbrokers little or no commission. As a result, it is mainly the much-despised private clients who have to hand over real money for their dealings. In 1990, 45% of all the commission revenue generated on UK shares came from individuals, those people the brokers grumble are too much trouble. The surprising thing to my mind is that even as far back as 1983, before Big Bang was but a twinkle in the eyes of Cecil Parkinson and Sir Nicholas Goodison, private clients provided just a quarter of the value of UK equity dealings but still 46.4% of total commission revenue. How does that square with us subsidising the big boys?

Although we little people are small and fiddly to deal with, private clients generated a total of £540 million for their brokers in 1990. Not a bad figure for a group that most stockbrokers would apparently like to eradicate altogether. Back in 1987, the figure was as high as £620 million and may, indeed, exceed that figure in 1991 if the market continues to push to new peaks.

Question: What do you call a former stockbroker?
Answer: Waiter!

It is strange now to recall that during the height of stock market fever in 1987, most stockbrokers wished many investors would simply go away. With privatisation issues clogging up the settlement system and every man and his dog (and even the dog's fleas) wanting a piece of the action, it is hardly surprising that many private clients were getting short shrift. Some were told not to ring their brokers to ask for share prices, but to call those premium telephone services instead (with the brokers taking a proportion of the revenue from such calls). New clients found it almost impossible to sign up with a stockbroker in some areas unless they were 'high net worth' individuals – what you or I would call stinking rich.

Now that business is back to more normal levels, the situation for new clients has improved considerably, although those brokers who believed the boom times were here to stay and who planned ahead accordingly must be feeling a bit yellow around the gills now. There is a wide variety of services on offer and those brokers in the provinces, whose rents and salaries are some considerable way below the big City boys, can offer a much more competitive service. Whereas minimum commissions have risen as high as £50 in the case of some large firms within the Square Mile (with those giant buildings, shouldn't it be the Cubic Mile?), the average minimum around the country is £20 or £25, with a good many firms still charging just £15.

Although one or two of the most highly publicised cut-price deal-only services have long since closed down, the victims of their own success and the inability of the brokers' back office systems to cope with that success, there are plenty left. Many investors new to the stock market pay too much attention to the price they are paying for their transactions. One of the best kept financial secrets over the past few decades has been the incredible all-round service given by stockbrokers. They have been one of the best sources of independent financial advice, have helped with tax, with school fees, with insurance, in fact with almost any investment-related matter an investor could bring to them. Frequently, such help has been given without the broker benefiting in any way, apart from improving the goodwill between him and the client. The Financial Services Act, and the costs that bob along in its considerable wake, may persuade some brokers to begin charging for things that have hitherto been gratis but the general principle still holds true.

Yet the individual who opts for the deal-only service cuts himself off from all of this. He can dial his broker, give an order and that's his lot. Start quizzing the chap on the other end of the line about Capital Gains Tax indexation relief and he will get pretty short shrift. These services can indeed be very valuable but investors who are still feeling their way tentatively in the stock market may do better to pay a little more for the security of having somebody to hold their hand.

The investment wizard who knows his own mind may very sensibly feel that the cheaper the dealing, the greater the return, and use the most reasonable service on offer. That makes perfect sense.

Unless you feel a compelling urge to visit your stockbroker for a chat over tea and biscuits, it doesn't really matter where in the country your broker is based. Providing you find one with whom you are happy, it may be a false economy to cut him for the sake of a few pounds less per deal. This is particularly true for investors who deal relatively rarely and who rely, not on their skill in making quick turns, but instead on the soundness of their investment choices, or those of their broker, to provide them with increasing capital and income.

Having waxed lyrical about the excellent breadth of services offered by stockbrokers, I think it only fair to point out that the whole atmosphere pervading the stock market over the past few years has changed markedly. It is no longer sensible to take too many things on trust. The changes wrought by Big Bang, the costs and complications of complying with the Financial Services Act, the boom in brokers' wage packets and the influx of many investors unused to the ways of the Stock Exchange have undermined the old informal relationship between stockbroker and client. It is, perhaps, a little surprising that so much was left unsaid in the old days. Nostalgic buffers like me can't help getting dewy-eyed thinking of those halcyon days, just a few years ago.

I wonder if someone ought not to report the Stock Exchange to the Advertising Standards Authority over the words adorning its crest of arms, 'Dictum Meum Pactum'.

After visiting one of his clients, a wealthy retired colonel on the south coast, a stockbroker decides to get a bit of fresh air before returning to the office. He takes a stroll along the cliff top but, to his horror, the ground gives way beneath his feet and he suddenly finds himself falling through the air.

He grabs hold of a tree root and hangs dangling over a drop of several hundred feet. In desperation, he calls out: 'Is there anybody up there? Is there anybody up there?'

To his surprise, there is a response. It comes, however, not from the top of the cliff, but from the heavens. 'Who is that?' the broker asks in amazement.

'God,' booms the reply.

'Save me,' pleads the broker.

'Certainly,' says God. 'I will save you in return for agreeing to give up all your worldly goods. If you let go of the branch, I will ensure that you float gently to earth.'

'All my worldly goods? My house, my Porsche, my partnership?'

'Yes.'

'And I'll simply float to earth?'

'Yes. Like a feather.'

'How do I know I can trust you?'

'Of course you can trust me. It's well known that my word is my bond.'

'Oh no,' wailed the broker in dismay. 'Is there anybody else up there?'

The idea that the Exchange should still, in the post-Big Bang world, have as its motto 'My Word is My Bond' is a little ludicrous. Perhaps they should change it to 'My tape-recording is my bond.' We live in an increasingly litigious world and hordes of lawyers now infest the fabric of the Stock Exchange, as they do so many other walks of life.

Despite the advent of the Financial Services Act, you

should still keep a very close watch on the ideas proposed by your stockbroker or, indeed, by any financial adviser. They are under an obligation of the FSA to give 'best advice.' Yet they are also likely to consider what benefit they will derive from recommending a particular course of action. Insurance-based products are likely to have a very much higher level of commission payment, for instance, than pure investment in stocks and shares. Stockbrokers are terribly fond of telling small investors that, with the funds they have at their disposal, they cannot possibly hope to get a wide enough range of investments. That may well be true, but to go on from there to recommend unit trusts may have more to do with the 3% introductory commission than the investor's best interests. Someone buying investment trusts instead, which are similar to unit trusts, except that they are quoted companies, would pay only ordinary stockbroker's commission and so would be less lucrative.

Of course, an investor wanting unit trust can go directly to the management group concerned. Some investment trusts are now realising the sense of operating in this way and offer savings schemes to investors who can opt either to buy a particular number of shares in one fell swoop or else start up a regular savings scheme. The commission levels on these are particularly low. An investor buying an investment trust through a stockbroker may have to pay 1.65% with a minimum cost of £20 or £25, if not more. Some of the investment trust groups would charge nothing more than 0.2%, a pretty big difference. Management charges also tend to be a fraction of those levied by unit trusts, making it little wonder that, over the years, investment trust returns have beaten not only building societies and insurance bonds, but unit trusts as well, and by a handsome margin too. Investment trusts are often the most sensible way into the stock market for a new investor, particularly someone who otherwise only owns a privatisation share or two. If a professional financial adviser doesn't even mention them to you, you should ask yourself why and possibly even report him. We aren't still at school any more; sneaks don't get beaten up whenever teacher turns her back. (A list of those investment trusts that offer savings schemes and direct investment are available from the Association of Investment Trust Companies on 071–588 5347.)

There aren't many stockbrokers among those boasting about the wonders of the privatisation programme. More problems have been caused by this than almost anything else in the Stock Exchange's history. It isn't only the sheer volume of dealings in the early days of a privatised company's life on the Stock Exchange or the settlement problems that result from it that infuriates them or the fact that so many people coming into contact with a stockbroker for the first time have so little idea what to expect. Much of their fury is reserved for the Treasury, and here many private investors will be wholly in agreement, for allocating such paltry numbers of shares in so many of the privatisations. Despite the furore on earlier issues, just 100 shares were handed out to most public applicants in British Airports Authority, now known hideously as BAA, in July 1987.

As anyone who has tried it will know, persuading a stockbroker you have never encountered before to sell just £145-worth of shares is not the easiest thing in the world to do. It ranks somewhere in the list of man's achievements alongside the conquest of Everest or the 4-minute mile. It is no wonder that many stockbrokers simply didn't want to know and no wonder that between July 1987 and May 1988, when the second call was due on the shares, over a million

Investors are often puzzled by the way in which shares in new issues are allotted to applicants.

The element of discrimination against the man in the street which some are convinced takes place is certainly not new, according to the history of stockbroker Helbert Wagg.

A partner, A R Wagg, wrote about a very successful new issue the firm handled at the turn of the century. 'It was on behalf of a well-known firm of provision merchants. Applications were on an enormous scale, and I have always understood that the company's chairman insisted on personally making the allotments.

'Dukes and Marquises were allotted in full. Earls, Viscounts and Barons received 50 per cent, Baronets and Honourables 25 per cent, and the general members of the public, nil.

'I believe a certain number of Society beauties were considered as ranking equally with Dukes and Marquises for the purposes of allotment. Needless to say, the shares went to a substantial premium.'

of the initial applicants had dumped their holdings. Similar pathetic bundles of shares were handed out to applicants in issues like Britoil, Rolls-Royce, the water companies, the electricity companies and so many others. In many cases investors had taken the advice given in the advertising and pre-registered an interest, being led to believe that this entitled them to preferential treatment. Far from receiving preferential treatment, they got fobbed off with tiny holdings that are no use to man nor beast. By insisting on such ludicrous allocations again and again, the Treasury only reinforces the view in many peoples' minds that you need hardly any money at all to get involved in the stock market.

You don't have to be a Rothschild, but you do need some real money. You can invest in investment trust savings schemes for as little as £20 a month but if you want to invest directly in shares, then £500 is the least you can consider for each holding. Stockbrokers aren't in the business they are because there were already too many donkey sanctuaries or childrens' charities. They are there to make money and while many will be willing to take on relatively small clients in the hope that they will grow over the years, anyone making it clear that all they want to do is sell their holding in TSB or British Gas and that's your lot is unlikely to find the red carpet laid underfoot.

In the language of market-makers quoting the size in which they are willing to deal on the Stock Exchange SEAQ system, 50×25 means they are willing to buy 50,000 and to sell 25,000 at the prices quoted.

One market-maker believed that he had been the victim of some sharp practice by his competitors in one share and immediately adjusted his entry to read simply: 5H×1T. The message was easily understood by his rivals.

There are one or two bright spots on the horizon for the private investor. By the time this book comes out, the Stock Exchange ought, if it holds good to its plans, to have introduced a new system with the snazzy name of SAEF. This stands for SEAQ Automatic Execution Facility, which may make you none the wiser unless you know that SEAQ is the Stock Exchange's share price information service, the video terminals of which sit on every stockbroker's desk. Despite the name, SEAF is not a system which immediately executes by electrocution any broker who dares to transgress the rules – the Financial Services Act isn't quite that draconian – but is for transacting orders in a thousand shares or less automatically. Restricted to shares in the larger companies, all a broker need do when given a client's order is press a couple of buttons on a keypad and, hey presto, the deal is carried out electronically at the best price shown on the SEAQ system. Isn't it a wonderful innovation?

Before too long we should see the introduction of TAURUS, which aims to do away with much of the paperwork involved in the transfer of ownership of shares. Instead of share certificates, supposedly unhackable computers will record who owns what. The date for the introduction of TAURUS has been put back so many times that I would not dream of suggesting when it might actually begin to operate. The Government promised that stamp duty on share purchases would be abolished at the same time, but the Chancellor probably made this promise with his tongue firmly in his cheek, knowing that this particular carrot would not need to be pulled out of the ground for some considerable time.

Just think how technology has changed the lives of stockbrokers in only a few short years. The abandonment of the Stock Exchange floor meant no more tiresome trudging around between jobbers to find out what prices they were making in the individual shares. Instead they now sit comfortably in their ergonomically designed chairs in air-conditioned offices.

It only remains to be asked why, if brokers aren't needed for bargaining on the price of investments on behalf of private clients or for coping with problems caused by the transfer of lots of redundant bits of paper, they are needed at all? Can't we have a system whereby credit-vetted individuals can tap their buying and selling orders into the system themselves, or is that a very skilled job?

Wanted: Stockbroker to look after small private clients

Lord Roll, the chairman of merchant bank Warburgs, made a tongue in cheek prediction at the beginning of 1988, suggesting that 'a strong rumour will persist in the City that the Government is shortly to introduce legislation banning all electronic equipment, including pocket calculators, in foreign exchange dealing rooms, and imposing the compulsory use of the abacus. This, it is said, would slow down foreign exchange dealings sufficiently to make exchange rates less volatile.'

Although he may have had his tongue firmly in his cheek at the time, it sounds eminently sensible to me.

A stockbroker of considerable standing gave me his own reason to explain the jittery nature of stock markets these days. 'It's quite simple. The volatility of the stock market is in direct proportion to the number of Topic sets. It is simply too emotive seeing prices in red and blue. People didn't work themselves up into such a lather when the prices were in rather fuzzy black and white on the old system.'

In fact, in America, the discount brokerage house, Charles Schwab is trying out just such a system, called Telebroker, which allows clients to buy and sell shares by pressing buttons on their telephone, the president of the company referring to it as 'the automatic teller machine of the brokerage business.' After giving an identification number, you can deal, find out share prices, or get details of your account. You pay no more for the service (I should think not) but Schwab's estimate that the cost to them is one-tenth of that of using a real human being or even, failing that, a stockbroker (Satire! Whatever next?). Schwab's have two million customers in the United States, so if the experiment is successful, presumably it can't be too long before it crosses the Atlantic.

There could also be clearing houses with which investors

who want to buy or sell particular shares at particular prices can register their requirements. Any investor tapping in and seeing an attractive share offered at the right price, or someone wanting to buy a share he owns, could press a few buttons and the deal is done. Perhaps stockbrokers will, in a decade or so, have gone the way of the dinosaur or the hula-hoop? I think that, at the very least, London Zoo ought to preserve one or two in captivity before they become extinct. But then I am a bit of a sucker for nostalgia and the good old days.

4

My Word is My Bond (tee, hee!)

The Stock Exchange is firmly in favour of wider share ownership. Isn't it always saying so? Isn't it also an organisation which boasts proudly that its merest word should be taken as binding?

How strange, then, that so many of the Exchange's actions over the past years have seemed to work to the detriment of private investors and to the benefit of the institutional investor.

Take, for instance, its decision to ban companies coming to the stock market from putting pictures relating to their business (or to anything else) in their prospectuses, except on the outside cover. Their concern is that while figures cannot lie (a dangerous and fallacious assumption to make) the camera apparently can. Perhaps a former chairman of the Stock Exchange, Sir Nicholas Goodison, feels that the photographs published of him over the years have done scant justice to his movie-star looks. Whatever the reason, that is now the rule: no photos except on the cover.

The idea that the majority of investors can plough through the figures contained in a prospectus and gain

It is extraordinary what you come across in the stock market reports in the newspapers. This appeared in the middle of the *Daily Telegraph*'s market report one day:

'Wall Street's better opening prompted a recovery in oil shares. **British Petroleum** ended just 6 off at 915p, **Shell** 7 lower at £12.16, and **Britoil** a shade easier at 241p. Elsewhere **Ewing Oil** were a bright spot and jumped 20 to 295p as bid speculation heightened. The word in the market is that cash-rich West Star has managed to pick up 10 p.c. of the tightly-held shares and is about to launch a full bid. **Goal Petroleum** were unchanged at 78p following the results.'

The date was April 1st, a fact that *Dallas* viewers were likely to cotton onto before the rest of the paper's readers.

more than a glimmer of the state of a business is ludicrous in itself. It should be enough that the various accountants, lawyers and the Stock Exchange have permitted a company to come to market. Should any porkies have been told, surely the hordes of advisers on the issue will be held responsible. Investors are more interested in knowing what sort of business it is in, what its prospects are for the years ahead and what the rest of the investment community's attitude towards it is likely to be. For this, comments in the financial press are invaluable. The ability of the newspapers to gauge the temperature of the water that a new issue is about to dive into is pretty good.

The thought that investors will allow themselves to be swayed into investing in an issue simply because of a few pretty pictures is akin to the Stock Exchange admitting that we are half-witted imbeciles who should not be allowed anywhere near a share. Their concern was apparently sparked off by issues like Laura Ashley and the Really Useful Group, whose prospectuses could have graced even the most superior of coffee tables, so lavishly bedecked with photographs were they.

I am not sure that I can see anything wrong with that. On the contrary, I believe that pictures can help investors to make up their minds about a company. It can be very useful to be able to see what the board of directors look like and to get a glimpse of the firm's plants and its products. In the case of companies involved in design, advertising and marketing, the photos can be all important; how can you make a judgment without seeing some examples of the work they have done?

Let it not be thought, however, that everybody suffers from the same disadvantages when it comes to new issues. Are the institutions shielded from dangerous visions of the company in the same way as mere private investors? Is the Pope Jewish? Is the moon made of blue cheese? The institutions may well get taken to the company's headquarters or its main plant before the flotation to meet the board and to quiz them about the way they run their business. There may even be videos produced for those who don't go on such a trip (imagine a video without any pictures – what use would that be?) or glossy corporate brochures.

The institutions can see all they need to before a new issue comes to market. Private investors can get but the barest glimpse. This is such a stupid rule as to almost beggar belief. If such a lot of work goes into checking and double checking the figures contained in a prospectus, can't some effort go into checking any photographs included, so that companies have to include pictures relating to their own business and not the far more successful factory over the road?

After all, Annual Reports are now stuffed chock-full of

photos. Even companies like GEC, which stuck to its bland, no-nonsense, no illustrations, policy as long as it could, now goes for the glossy treatment. Most reports now have pictures of company directors leering out at shareholders from every nook and cranny (some go a great deal too far and ought to consider putting bags over their directors' heads), of happy employees hard at work, of presses and production lines running flat out and of consumers snapping up the firm's products as if there were no tomorrow. All this is perfectly legal. Boards of directors aren't, as I write, languishing at Her Majesty's Pleasure because they dared to show shareholders such pernicious and seditious material. On the contrary, companies realise how essential it is to let those investors who can't meet them and visit their plants in person see what they look like.

Yet thanks to the Stock Exchange, investors have to make their decisions on whether to invest in a new issue partly blindfolded. Only once their money has been committed, and the first Annual Report arrives from the company, will investors find the blindfold taken from their eyes.

As in so many other areas, privatisation issues are a little different. People registering interest in these will find themselves the recipient of pretty brochures brimming over with photographs. Admittedly they are not in the prospectus itself, but that's a pretty narrow distinction to make, if you ask me.

For the majority of investors interested in new issues, one of the most serious problems faced is not what is contained within the prospectus, but how to get hold of one at all. There is very little time between the final announcement of a flotation and the date on which applications have to be received. The larger new issues will issue complete prospectuses (without any photographs) in at least a couple of national newspapers, but the rules for the rest have been relaxed considerably over the past few years. It is possible now for a relatively modest new issue, even an offer for sale, to get away with issuing only a very small announcement. Those few square inches will contain an application form, but very few details about the company. Ever mindful of the need to protect the public, the advisers to the issue will warn that potential investors should do nothing before reading the full listing particulars.

These will be made available in the offices of some of the financial advisers handling the sale. This is no doubt fine if you live in London, or perhaps Manchester, Edinburgh, Glasgow or one or two other cities and have the time to spend in arranging to pick up a copy of the prospectus. What about the rest of the population? With less than a week between the appearance of the advertisements and the closing date for applications (which always warn that two working days should be allowed for first class post to arrive), this would not allow time for anybody to write in asking for full details. Telephoning might just get a prospectus to you in time but the rules do not compel advisers to insert any such useful phone numbers in their adverts. Still, why change the way things are done now? Anybody in the Square Mile can easily stroll around for a prospectus in their lunch hour. As for the rest of the populace, who cares? The City boys certainly don't.

New issues are, of course, the most common way for investors to buy shares. Apparently almost four-fifths of all shares held by individuals in this country have been bought when the companies first came to the market, primarily in the government sell-offs. You would imagine, perhaps, that it would be a good idea to ensure that the new issue market is made as widely accessible to private investors as possible? If so, you reckon without the wisdom of the Stock Exchange.

THE SHAREHOLDER

One hundred years ago a few members of the Stock Exchange printed a little volume reflecting the humour of nineteenth-century stockbrokers, *House Scraps*. It was reprinted recently by Abbey Unit Trust managers in an enlightened moment.

Amongst the many gems it contains is this cod ad from October 25th 1845, a time when railway mania gripped the nation and applying for new issues reached a popularity not seen again until the 1980s.

TO THE STAGGING WORLD

Messrs. Nathan beg to inform their friends and the public that they have fitted up extensive premises opposite the Exchange, where costumes of every description likely to inspire confidence will be hired out to gents intending to sign for railway scrip in two or more characters, at a very low figure.

LIST OF PRICES

	£	s	d
Bishop's costume – apron, hat, black silks and buckles	1	1	0
Low Church Rector – black tights, short gaiters, &c; false calves if required	0	15	0
Puseyite Divine – long black single-breasted coat, narrow collar	0	10	6
Sporting Banker of the Old School – blue coat, brass buttons, yellow waistcoat, drab pants, or shorts	0	15	0
Watch chain and bunch of seals, extra	0	5	0
Flash West-End Gent – cutaway coat, velvet vest, railway pants	0	15	0
Mosaic jewellery for ditto	0	5	0
Country Gents, Widows, KCBs and Comfortable Tradesmen got up at five minutes' notice in the most accurate manner, each	0	10	6

My Word is My Bond (tee, hee!)

The new issue market was pretty healthy in 1988, particularly when one considers that it was fairly drastically curtailed by the Crash. The number of sales raising fresh capital grew from 58 in 1985 to 66. Yet as far as private investors were concerned, the number of new issues for which they could apply actually shrank sharply.

Back in 1985, 91% of all those new issues that raised fresh capital were the traditional offers for sale, with advertisements in newspapers enabling potential investors to cut out a coupon and send it in with a cheque. The rest were placings, exercises in which the stockbroker sponsoring the company hands out shares to favoured clients, giving most private investors no chance to buy before trading begins.

	New Issues Raising Cash (excluding USM)				
	Offers for sale		Placings		Total
1985	54	93%	6	7%	60
1988	12	18%	54	82%	66

SOURCE: PEAT MARWICK MCLINTOCK

Late in 1986, the Stock Exchange changed its rules on new issues. It increased the limit that could be raised through such placings five-fold, from £3m to £15m. As a minimum of 25% of shares must be sold when a company seeks a listing on the main market, this means that firms with a market capitalisation as high as £60m can now opt for the placing route. As this is far cheaper than an offer for sale and as the company's advisers feel it an advantage to be able to control the distribution of shares and ensure that they go into friendly hands, it is hardly surprising that the number of placings has shot up.

From only 5 in 1985, the figure in 1988 was 54. The number of offers for sale shrank from 53 to a bare 12. Private investors were thus effectively barred from participating in over 80% of all new issues on the main stock market in 1988.

The Unlisted Securities Market is a gloomier prospect still, with few new issues of any sort and almost none of them offers for sale. However, although the Stock Exchange changed the USM rules at the same time as those for the main market, it is perhaps only fair that small companies in the early days of their life should be able to opt for an entry route to the stock market that does not carry with it crippling costs.

The same cannot be said of the main market. Placings do not help to spread the ownership of shares very widely. The Stock Exchange's rule that for every £1m raised through a placing there should be at least 30 names on the

---

When the scientist Albert Einstein departed this mortal coil, he found himself in heaven. But bureaucracy being as much of a problem there as on earth, he was told to wait on a nearby cloud by a rather officious gatekeeper.

There were three other angels-to-be there, also waiting to be processed. The great man drifted into conversation with them.

'Hello,' he greeted the first. 'I am Albert Einstein. Do you know what your IQ is?' '180,' was the reply.

'Splendid,' said Einstein. 'Then we will be able to have many interesting conversations about my fascinating theory of relativity, about the mechanics of time and about the nature of the universe.'

In like manner, he quizzed the second person, to be told that his IQ was 135.

'Good,' said Einstein. 'I am sure that we will be able to discuss art, music and the great literary figures of the past.'

Einstein then turned to the third chap and asked, 'What is your IQ?' '60,' he was told.

'Ah,' said Einstein. 'And how's the market today?'

---

share register is a pathetic sop to People's Capitalism. New issues are the main method for many investors of buying shares. Despite the fact that offers for sale are more expensive than placings, surely helping to extend the breadth of share ownership is a price worth paying?

The planned ending of the century-old Account system is another example of the Stock Exchange ignoring the wishes of private clients and their brokers and listening instead only to the big boys, the institutions and the securities houses who service them. The present Stock Exchange Account is beneficial to the private investor in more ways than one. It enables investors to buy and sell the same shares without actually having to find the money for the initial transaction, as only the difference between the purchase and sale price has to be settled at the end of the Account. But it also allows for the rearrangement of portfolios and for switching which can be done over a two or three week period. Instead of lots of small bills or repayments, there is only one for each account.

Although the Exchange claims that this can lead to settlement problems, more than one private client broker has told me that the Account system actually minimises financial and administrative complications for both broker and investor. Around 15% of Stock Exchange transactions are for the Account. For many retail-orientated brokers the figure will be substantially higher. Although not all of this business will disappear completely with the ending of the Account, a reduction in the general level of business could well have the effect of forcing brokers to increase their charges or postponing the date when they decrease them.

The Exchange has a rather ambivalent attitude to speculators. I get the impression that at times it almost wishes they would go away, so much embarassment do they seem to cause the prim and proper gentlemen (no ladies, of

course) who govern the affairs of that great establishment. Yet as every student of economics knows (if he has been paying attention), speculators bring liquidity to markets. This is as true of those who trade within the Account as anyone else. Without their wheelings and dealings, activity in a great many shares will undoubtedly be reduced, with a probable widening of spreads by market-makers to compensate.

We may be moving towards 24-hour Global Markets, but there can still be problems with language, even between nations that supposedly speak the same tongue.

The Chicago Board of Trade, who run a thriving options and futures exchange, began a contract based upon the UK's FTSE-100 Share Index. They publicised this in the UK, sending out not only a press release, but also their latest Annual Report.

On its cover was a hand demonstrating the sign that Chicago traders use to indicate that they want to buy or sell two contracts. Unfortunately, the gesture with the two erect fingers has a quite different meaning in Britain!

The Stock Exchange gives a couple of reasons for wanting to move to a rolling Account system, with settlement always five days ahead of the current day, possibly being reduced to three later on. It will, apparently, lessen the risk of default in another market crash, an argument much akin to that of the person wanting to abolish motorways in the wake of a pile-up.

The other is to bring ourselves into line with other major markets around the world who have rolling settlements. Why, for goodness sake? We should be exporting our splendid Account system, not abolishing it. The next thing you know someone will be telling us we have to drive on the right hand side of the road, simply because that's the way the foreigners do it!

I can at least understand the Stock Exchange's irritation with the decision by the Securities and Investments Board that the new compensation funds brought in by the Financial Services Act should operate on an industry-wide basis. Instead of stockbrokers only being responsible if another stockbroker goes phut, they may now have to dig their hands into their pockets if the proprietor of some seedy back street financial intermediary decamps to the Bahamas with his secretary and all his clients' cash.

The new compensation fund covering all investment advisers provides 100% compensation up to £30,000 and then 90% of the next £20,000, for a total of £48,000. The Stock Exchange, in its wisdom, decided that it could not contribute to this and have its own fund operating too, so it junked its old system. This was something of a pity, as the Stock Exchange compensation scheme had protected investors' funds up to £250,000, or even £500,000 in some cases. It was this compensation fund which made so many investors feel perfectly secure in handing considerable sums of money over to stockbrokers to look after. The chaps may have no chins and drive around in flash cars, but at least their peers would have to cough up if their firm kicked the bucket. Fewer than 20 Stock Exchange firms have gone under since 1973, most in a spate of defaults at the time of the '74 bear market. Despite the Crash of '87, only half a dozen or so have handed in their meal ticket in the past decade. Not a bad record, and every investor who lost out as a result was compensated.

Those investors who use their broker only to transact deals will not be too badly affected. There can't be many of us with orders outstanding for more than £50,000 at a time.

But in the wake of the appalling settlement problems of 1987, an increasing number of firms are encouraging clients to use their nominee services. Sensible though this may be, it exposes the investor with over £50,000 to risks on his entire portfolio in the event of a default by the stockbroker. Those whose portfolio is managed by a broker, but who have the shares correctly registered in their own name will not be affected as the securities are obviously their property.

Another problem with the SIB scheme is that you are not even absolutely guaranteed to get back £48,000 on your £50,000 in the event of default. If there is a terrible year, with financial advisers going down like ninepins, then any claims may be scaled back. It is planned that the fund have a total value in any one year of £100 million. Although that may sound like a lot, if it is exceeded, those who have already been paid out on claims earlier in the year may find themselves having to pay some of it back.

Only 0.5% of claims on the Stock Exchange's compensation fund since 1973 were above £50,000 (14% in value), so it should not have been too expensive for the Exchange to have continued it in some form. By abolishing it, they have thrown a considerable amount of goodwill out of the window as well. Now, if someone wants to entrust their portfolio to a stockbroker, they may think twice about letting them have any more than £50,000 to look after. The trouble is, of course, that most broking firms won't take anyone on who gives them any less than that. Catch-22.

One very small victory for the private investor is the decision to abandon a new levy on all Stock Exchange dealings imposed in January 1987. As most investors who have dealt since then will know, any deal for more than £1,000 incurred a charge of 80 pence, with 30 pence of this going to help run the Takeover Panel and 50 pence going to the Securities and Investments Board in membership fees for the Stock Exchange and The Securities Association. However, not all members of The Securities Association conduct business on The Stock Exchange and so it was decided to do away with the new levy in March 1989. From then on, as far as the investor is concerned, it is back to the old system, with 60 pence levied on share bargains above £5,000 to help the running costs of the Panel. However, as The Securities Association decided to raise its fees by 15% to compensate for the loss of the new levy, presumably the increased costs will eventually find their way back to the investors. They usually do.

Although, in my opinion, there are more disadvantages than advantages resulting from the Financial Services Act, at least from the stock market investor's point of view, the new capital adequacy requirements, expensive though they may be for brokers to operate, will make the risk of any stockbroker going belly up considerably less likely. Investors will probably be more at risk from fraud and negligence and the majority of brokers are likely to have insured against this. One leading private client stockbroker has an 'In and Out' policy against fraud on the part of its directors and employees. Clients losing money as a result of this are covered up to two million pounds each. The firm has similar cover against claims arising from negligence.

There was a time when I steered anybody with a substantial sum of money to invest towards a bona-fide stockbroker, a member of the Stock Exchange. Your money

---

Question: What do you give the stockbroker who has everything for Christmas?

Answer: Five years.

---

could not have been safer (allowing for the vagaries of the market). Now that the compensation fund is so pitifully small, it is hard to be so confident. Perhaps investors who are keen to make sure their money is not going to disappear in a puff of smoke should only use those stockbrokers who stick to 'agency' business. In the post-Big Bang era, not every firm makes markets in stocks and shares. Many, if not most, private client firms only transact business on

Although the majority of traders have now departed the Stock Exchange floor for ever, the Traded Options dealers who remain try their best to keep alive the spirit of joie de vivre which once thrived in those hallowed halls.

Although the Stock Exchange no longer regards the admission of television cameras to the floor of the House with horror, those still working there are not quite so keen on the intrusion of strangers.

An Australian camera crew lasted little more than ten minutes beneath a hail of rolled-up newspapers, while a Japanese crew had to retreat almost as soon as they arrived.

They were much more polite to a British camera crew, to the relief of the female TV reporter doing part of her story from the Stock Exchange floor. She had been prepared for trouble but, far from being boisterous, the traders appeared on the contrary to be extremely quiet and well-behaved.

Came the moment when she was ready to do her piece in front of the camera and she was somewhat discomforted to find the camera crew doubled up with laughter. Unbeknownst to her, the grinning traders had quietly lined up behind her in the manner of schoolchildren preparing for their annual photograph!

What a far cry from the old days of the crowded floor when, if strangers appeared in the House, a cry of 'Fourteen Hundred' would go up and an intruder would be lucky to escape with his trousers intact.

behalf of their clients, not for themselves. The risks involved are obviously substantially lower. The risks involved for their clients are commensurately lower.

Despite proclaiming itself in favour of wider share ownership, there are times when I wonder if the Exchange really believes that individuals are to be trusted with shares of their own or whether it considers us all half-wits incapable of looking after our own affairs. This view was reinforced when the Stock Exchange gallery was reburbished and new aids to understanding what the stock market is all about were introduced. The necessity for them is even more crucial now that there is nothing to see on the floor except for the Traded Options dealers, conveniently hidden for the most part *underneath* the visitors' gallery.

There, the excited pupils can learn all about the Stock Exchange through a host of electronic machines, guided by the Stock Exchange's own 'exclusive cartoon character', Investor-Cat.

'No-one,' so we are told, 'suspected that the prim, demure, modest Cynthia in the buying department, was, in fact, an Investor-Cat! She stands for truth, justice and making money on the stock market! Yes . . . she's an Investor-Cat.'

Investor-Cat's message to all you punters everywhere is: 'Don't Nest It . . . Invest It!' For those who want to spread the word as widely as possible, you can even buy a T-shirt proclaiming that very thing. A snip at £7.50! Who says the Stock Exchange isn't helping to encourage wider share ownership! Not I.

5

Whose Company Is It Anyway?

The behaviour of some (if not the majority of) companies towards their shareholders sometimes defies belief, so offhand and dismissive is it. There ought to be a law passed compelling every company director in the land to have a notice five-foot high facing his desk reading: 'It isn't your company, chum. It belongs to the shareholders, and don't you forget it.'

Many chief executives persist in treating the firms for which they work as their own personal fiefdoms, showing themselves to their small shareholders just once a year at the Annual General Meeting and rushing the whole business through as quickly as possible so that they can disappear off for lunch with their fellow directors, leaving the shareholders behind with nothing but a cup of nasty coffee and a couple of biscuits.

As far as I am concerned, directors come in three types. There are those who have been involved with the company for many years, since its inception perhaps, who own a substantial portion of the company's equity, and who, as larger investors themselves, obviously have the interests of the shareholders at heart. Then there are those who have come into the business as professional managers but who, because they have acquired a considerable number of shares over the years, can still identify with shareholders' interests. The other group, the sort I dislike the most, are those directors who own few or even no shares in the company for which they work, particularly if they treat the firm as if it were their own. How much confidence can an investor have if the directors themselves aren't willing to commit their own capital to the company?

Being a shareholder may bar you from carrying out your stint of jury service. Early in 1988, jurors in a bugging case involving Dixons and Woolworths were asked whether they held shares in either company before being allowed to take the oath.

This is an interesting precedent. A case involving the commercial interests of British Gas could exclude three million possible people from the jury!

In law, of course, directors are appointed by shareholders, on whose behalf they run the business, however much they may prefer to forget it. Every election to the board has to be approved by a resolution at the Annual General Meeting and directors have to stand for re-election every three years. Despite this apparent resemblance to the democratic process of government, we are usually given very little information indeed about these people. As the Bank of England recently pointed out, companies don't have to give details of the skills or experience of board members, nor even of their functions within the business. Some firms do so, but the number is pretty small. By law, all an Annual Report has to show is the names of the directors, their remuneration and their financial interests in the company. The one time investors will be given a good deal of information about the people running a quoted company is when it first comes to market. After that, unless you attend the AGM, you may never get an idea of what they are really like. This makes it extremely difficult to know what to do when asked to vote on the election or re-election of directors, particularly as it is almost always the existing board who suggest the appointment of any newcomers.

The practice of appointing non-executive directors can work as a restraint upon the main board, particularly if they are high-powered people in their own right. However, about half of all large companies have only one or two non-execs and, unless they are men (or possibly women) who are far from the shy and retiring type, it is hard to imagine them creating much of a stir if the board are about to do something stupid, particularly if they need the retainer the company pays them. Many, in fact, will be chums of the existing board members or perhaps even ex-board members themselves. They're hardly likely to rock the boat excessively on any occasion when it deserves a good shaking about. Gracious, no. They might lose a good golfing partner!

Ticking the 'no' box on your proxy card to vote against the appointment of a particular director simply because you don't like his name or photograph or because you think the whole board are a bunch of over-paid deadbeats who wouldn't last ten minutes on the production line may be satisfying, but it won't get you very far. Interestingly, this is one area where the small investor can exercise a little power. Ask the company for a copy of its Articles of Association, setting out the rules under which it operates. For a shareholder to propose a resolution to be put before the Annual General Meeting usually needs either a minimum of a twentieth of the voting capital of the company behind it, or the backing of at least a hundred shareholders, each having paid up an average of £100.

The difficulties of getting such support make individual shareholders' resolutions a fairly rare event. To dismiss a director before his term of office comes to an end, for instance, needs an ordinary resolution. So unless you have 99 buddies who have a similar lack of admiration for a particularly incompetent director, you can do little but stick your tongue out at him from your vantage point in the front row at the AGM.

However, despite the considerable amount of support you will need to canvass to get an ordinary resolution put before the Annual General Meeting, it is possible (Articles of the company permitting) that you will need only one other shareholder to propose you (or anyone else) as a director of the company. This too is an option that seems to be utilised only very rarely. It is a wonder that the Monster Raving Loony Party and other political(?) organisations of their ilk have not yet cottoned onto the ease with which this can be done, particularly now that the size of deposits required for candidates at general and by-elections has been raised considerably.

Considering the amount of discussion in the press and elsewhere about the size of some directors' remuneration, it is staggering how little information on the subject is contained in the Annual Report. True, it has to list directors' pay, but it doesn't need to say who got what except for the highest-paid director and the chairman (which may or may not be the same thing).

Who decides how much directors should get paid? Why, they do of course. Many large companies profess to have independent remuneration committees deciding such weighty matters on which only non-executive directors are permitted to sit, but the idea that these committees will ever cut a director's pay savagely is laughable. Do that, and the next thing you know the non-executives will find their lunch allowances curtailed! The majority of non-executive directors are main board directors of other companies. If they were to take a stand against a director being paid handsomely, the next thing they knew, somebody might object when their own remuneration committee begins throwing telephone number salaries around.

In reality, directors' salaries only ever seem to go in one direction. Up.

Lyndsey Knight paid the bill for a meal he and a small group of friends were having in an Oxford restaurant. Deputy governor of the Reserve Bank of New Zealand, Knight was in the UK to attend a management conference.

When presented with the cheque, the waiter asked for proof of Knight's identity. He was handed a Bank of New Zealand note which, like all the others issued during his term as chief cashier, bore Knight's signature.

The waiter is reputed to have said: 'That really will do nicely, sir.'

No matter how 'troubled' the company, no matter what has happened to profits or earnings, no matter how desperate the plea to the workforce for restraint in pay bargaining, no matter how measly the dividend payout, directors' pay seems to rise inexorably. Whenever this subject is raised at AGMs (that's the trouble with private shareholders – they have no shame and will keep raising embarrassing topics), the reason usually given is that if the company is to have good directors running it, it must pay the going rate to secure and keep their services. In other words, because all other companies are pushing up their directors' pay so, sadly, must this one. This presumably keeps the momentum of the upward spiral going nicely. Sir John Clark, chairman of Plessey, increased his pay by a third to £298,206, according to the 1988 Annual Report, helping to boost his total remuneration package to a tidy £391,956. What a shame that Plessey's profits had fallen by 7% that year and that the company was soon to be taken over.

Companies that are privatised seem particularly ripe for massive increases in board remuneration. In its first full year as a private company, British Gas's chairman Sir Denis Rooke, received a modest pay rise from £74,228 to £183,674 while Lord King, chairman of British Airways, was given an increase from £52,000 to £178,000. Iain Vallance, replacing Sir George Jefferson as chairman of BT, had his salary upped from £153,000 to £226,000, even though the company had already been in the private sector for a couple of years. While Sir Denis's pay was going up by 68% at British Gas, the other directors were having to content themselves with a mere 40% rise. The non-executives must have been very disgruntled. Their pay rose by just 28%. It can hardly be worth their while turning up for meetings if they're only getting £9,000 a year.

Many companies claim that their directors' pay is performance-related but they are under no obligation, and usually feel no urge, to let shareholders know just how it is calculated. Usually it works out that if the company does moderately well, the main directors' pay soars into the stratosphere, whereas if the company's performance is lamentable, it rises by less than 50%. It is, however, still possible to come across directors whose pay does decline in a poor year. Sir Eric Sharp, chairman and chief executive of Cable and Wireless had to suffer a 20% pay cut to £208,000,

[74]

a slap on the wrist when Cable & Wireless's profits rose by a bare 5%.

A survey by Labour Research in 1990 showed that 14 British directors earned over a million pounds a year, while over 2,500 pulled in over £100,000 each. There used to be a time, in the dim, dark, distant days of supertaxes, when Annual Reports showed what directors got paid and then compared this, using graphs, to their post-tax position. Shareholders were presumably supposed to pity their directors' treatment at the cruel hand of the Chancellor of the Exchequer.

It isn't only in their level of pay that directors do so nicely, thank you. Whereas their production line workers or office staff toil knowing that they are on a week's or a month's notice, or possibly even three months', directors more and more commonly have service contracts under which their terms of service are two, three or possibly even five years. Heaven forbid that it should ever happen, but if a particular director were to get up the noses of the other board members sufficiently that he were to be kicked out of his job, he would be paid the money owing to him from the rest of his term in one lump sum. In some circumstances, he can resign and still get the money.

If companies decide to pay more to a director than he is entitled, then it must make sure that shareholders know what is going on. The Companies Act makes it unlawful for a company to make a payment as compensation for loss of office or in connection with retirement 'without particulars of the proposed payment (including its amount) being disclosed to members of the company and the proposal being approved by the company.'

Payments of compensation for loss of office are nothing like as gargantuan here as in the United States, where the ex-chairman of CBS received $11.4 million on his dismissal.

Poor John Barkshire, ex-chairman of Mercantile House, is said to have received less than a million pounds compensation, two directors of Morgan Grenfell a measly £562,000 between them, Sir Ronald Halstead of Beecham just £407,000 and Michael Newman of Britannia Arrow a paltry £400,000. Hardly enough to keep body and soul together. Plessey, incidentally, in the same year as it increased Sir John's pay, also shelled out just over a million pounds to former directors who had retired from office. According to the Annual Report, there were only three leavers in that year. Two directors of Storehouse, Denis Cassidy and Colin Williams, objected to the appointment of a managing director from outside the group. Their inability to resolve this little difficulty led to their resignations. One was on £120,000 a year with three years of his contract left to run. The other was on £70,000 with two years left. Their total compensation was £600,000.

Incidentally, just to show that not all companies are as free and loose with what is, after all, the shareholders' money, one large firm at least eschews service contracts. It is Hillsdown Holdings, one of the top hundred companies in Britain. Harry Solomon, the chairman, told me at a recent AGM that: 'I don't believe in service contracts. We have never had them and we never will. If the shareholders want to throw us out then they can. My directors would lay down their lives for this company and they don't need service contracts to protect them.'

The salary of a director is particularly important as he approaches retirement, because his pension will be linked to his final salary. Surprise, surprise, the board usually find it necessary to boost each other's pay as this calamitous day approaches so that by the time the gold watch is handed over to the chap his retirement can be made as comfortable as possible. Sir George Jefferson, for instance, retired as

chairman from British Telecom, with a pension and compensation package worth almost £900,000.

Of course, sometimes a pension just isn't enough for a man to retire on. It costs a fortune these days to buy yourself one of those sit-upon lawnmowers essential for gardening in your twilight years. Even so, many eyebrows were raised at the proposals by Rothmans in the Summer of 1988. Sir Robert Crichton-Brown, chairman for three-and-a-half years, was about to retire. His pay (emoluments was the word used – it sounds so much more refined, don't you think?) had risen from £230,000 the previous year to £298,000 and he wanted to retire 18 months before his service contract ran out. His deputy chairman decided that, despite contributing £141,000 to his personal pension, it simply wouldn't be enough (those lawnmowers really eat up the petrol you see) and that, in the light of the company's success under Sir Robert's leadership, he ought to be given a cheque for £750,000. The letter to shareholders argued that 'he has presided over a period of remarkable change in (Rothman's) fortunes. Under his leadership great problems have been overcome and fine results achieved with the Group now substantially re-shaped and its balance sheet transformed. Due in no small measure to his personal contribution the Group is now well poised to seek out and acquire or develop the other profit streams which are needed to supplement the core business. Against this background your Board believes that it is appropriate that he should receive special recognition of his achievements on behalf of the Group.' There are those who think that if a person does a job, his pay should be adequate remuneration and that paying somebody retrospectively for it is a little odd. I wonder how the 30,000 employees of Rothmans who also contributed in some small way to the company's profits felt about it.

It is comforting to know that directors are concentrating on the important matters of life. The finance director of an engineering company with a market capitalisation of three quarters of a billion pounds sent round the following memo to all its head office staff:

'It has been brought to the attention of the writer that coffee/other liquid has twice been spilt in the elevator. For the sake of good housekeeping/safety, open cups of coffee/refreshments must not be transported in the elevator. Breaking of this rule will result in summary dismissal. You are required to sign below as confirmation and understanding of this instruction.'

Although the rather extraordinary payment had to be approved by shareholders and although there was some fairly stiff criticism from investors, at least one MP and the Institute of Directors, the proposal was carried through. This was largely because the South African Rembrant group and Philip Morris of America held 70% of Rothman's equity. They were in favour of the motion and the board refused to allow those shareholders who had taken the trouble to turn up even to have a show of hands on the motion.

Responding to criticism of the payment, Mr David Montagu would not explain how the figure was arrived at but said that a sub-committee of non-executive directors had been unanimous in their decision. Mr Montagu took over the helm from Sir Robert and was quoted at the time as saying that his emoluments would be at least as great as Sir Robert's. Boy, it's tough at the top.

You may be interested to know just how many shares in his company Sir Robert Crichton-Brown held at that time. None. Not one, solitary, share. Like the other executive directors, of course, he had plenty of share options, some

[79]

400,000 on which he will have been able to make a profit of about £800,000, but no shares directly at all. Sir Robert was not alone in this. None of the executive directors of Rothmans held shares in the company at the time of that Annual Report to shareholders. Of the whole board only one, John W Mayo, a non-executive director, had any equity stake in the company, having 13,666 of the 'B' shares to his name.

That reminds me of one of the most amusing things I have come across at a recent Annual General Meeting. It was during the voting of the resolutions. Like obedient puppies, the various members of the board were putting up their hands to show that they were in favour of the various motions. An indignant shareholder got to his feet. 'How dare two of the directors raise their hands', he fumed, 'when the Annual Report shows clearly that they held no shares in the company and so have no entitlement to vote?' Indeed, it was true. They owned no stake in the company. Only those with ordinary voting shares may vote at a general meeting and that includes directors, just like other mortals. If a director is not required by the company's Articles of Association to have shares in the company, then the Articles will usually permit a director to attend and speak at the meeting, but that is all.

I think it ludicrous that directors are even permitted to serve unless they have at least some shares in the company. Yet Annual Report after Annual Report shows up directors, both executive and non-executive, who have no financial interest in the business other than their pay-cheques. I can think of one leading retailer where the chairman has no shareholding at all, despite having been on the board for three years! Look at a few sets of accounts and you will notice that even those directors who have no shares will have oodles and oodles of options.

Many firms warble on pompously about how useful

profit-sharing and employee share schemes are for boosting motivation, yet an appalling number seem to believe that such motivation should start and finish in the boardroom; it's carrots for the directors and sticks for the rest. There are three types of Inland Revenue approved schemes. The most popular, presumably because it can be applied to senior management only, is the one introduced in the 1984 Finance Act. This enables options to be granted on shares worth up to four times salary. 77% of directors in companies with turnover between £300m and £1,000m have such schemes, while a staggering 93% of those with sales over £1,000m reward their directors in this way. Most restrict the benefits to main board directors. The comparable figures for senior management as a whole are 38% and 70%, according to a study in late 1987.

Options are granted at the current market price and, during the requisite period, an option holder can exercise them at any time between three and ten years after being granted them, although there must be three years between each exercise. Providing these rules are followed, there is no income tax to pay on the gain. The value of these schemes took a bit of a knock in the 1988 Budget, when the Chancellor equalised the tax rates on income and capital. There is little point in sticking to the rules of the approved schemes if you will eventually be taxed just as if you have received the money as income. Previously, they had been able to escape income tax of 60%, paying CGT at the lower rate of 30%. Now, that attraction has disappeared. It may be that directors will prefer to get extra money in their pay packets in future, especially now that top rates of tax have been so sharply reduced. Or they may simply ignore the restraints imposed on the approved schemes.

The 1988 Budget was the second blow to strike many directors in a short period. Those firms a little slow off the

> It was clear in the aftermath of the Crash that, while the true global, 24-hour stock market may still be some way off, there is already a global market in jokes. The following appeared in newspapers on both sides of the Atlantic on the same day: 'What is the difference between a pigeon and a stockbroker?'
>
> Answer: 'The pigeon can still manage to put a deposit on a Porsche.'
>
> In fact, there was a subtle difference in the two versions. The American joke used a Mercedes instead.

mark to set up their option schemes found the three year limit fell late in 1987. Directors who had been rubbing their hands with glee just a few weeks earlier saw their paper fortunes crumble in that October's Crash, just days before they could exercise their options. Don't shed too many tears for them. The Crash still only put shares back to their level of early 1987. For most directors, there were still very substantial profits to be made.

As an example of how they work, Sir Ralph Halpern, former chairman of Burton Group, was granted options over 545,000 shares at 23p in 1981. He exercised them in May 1987. At the time, the shares were 321p. He sold all of them and, with a profit of £2.98 on each, made £1,624,100 profit. Unfortunately for hard-done-by Sir Ralph, the options were granted before the Finance Act of 1984 so he had to pay income tax on the profit.

Sir Ralph blazed a trail on share options, finding the restrictions placed by the 1984 Finance Act too miserly. He was able to obtain shareholder approval to exceed these considerably, getting options with a value on paper of £2.5m. The institutions (and many private investors) dislike option schemes that go beyond the 1984 rules because of the dilution of their own holdings that result. Their Investor Protection Committees try to restrict companies to issuing fewer options than the 1984 rules would allow. In Burton's case, the company had to achieve very strong earnings per share growth over five years for the options to come into effect. That did not happen and poor Sir Ralph left with a mere £2 million pay-off.

The most extraordinary gains on directors' options, however, seem to be made when the company is first floated. A study by a City law firm, Paisner & Co, shows that directors commonly grant themselves options a few months before flotation at prices that bear no relation to the price other investors are asked to pay soon afterwards. As long as the Inland Revenue agrees to the option price when it is granted, there seems nothing to restrain them from doing so, even though the equity of other shareholders is thereby diluted. In 1990 ABI Leisure Group was floated at 125p per share. The directors had been granted options at just 7.14p, a discount of 94%, just five months earlier. The directors of Seton Healthcare Group received options at between 22.5p and 62.5p from September 1988 to June 1990. In July 1990, the company was floated at 130p.

With their tongues firmly in their cheeks many companies claim that one of the major reasons for seeking a quote on the stock market is to encourage employee share ownership. Yet although the vast majority of firms have executive share options schemes, far fewer have schemes covering all their employees.

The Government have tried to push directors into being more generous. From 1992 companies can grant options to executives at a 15% discount to market price, but only if the company also has an approved all-employee incentive scheme, be it through profit-sharing or share options.

What infuriates me beyond belief is when directors take

up their options and sell the entire lot straight away, pocketing the profit. Do they have so little faith in their own abilities and the future of the company that they cannot take the risk of holding onto the shares for a time? There are times when I think that some directors regard shares in a completely different light from other investors, looking upon them not as an investment for the future, but instead as money, as cash, as their right and proper due for running the business.

Perhaps I shouldn't knock option schemes too much. Management obviously do need incentives if they are to keep their noses to the grindstone, their backs to the wheel, and their golf clubs in the cupboard. It is the staggering amount of directors' remuneration that I find so obscene. When you see some directors at AGMs, you wonder what on earth they do with all that cash. There they sit, clad in suits that look as though they were rejected by the local Oxfam shop, sporting haircuts that look as though their wives have had to help out with the pudding basin and scissors and wearing smiles that look as though everything is about to crumble into dust in front of their eyes. I can think of relatively few boards of directors that have actually inspired me with confidence at an Annual Meeting. The shabbier they are, the more I find myself wondering just what they do with their money.

I've mentioned before the amazing number of directors who don't feel the need to have any shares in the company. The majority do have an equity stake in the business, though. Some even (shock! horror! gasp!) use their own money for buying them in the market. There are restrictions on when directors can, and cannot, deal in the shares of the company for which they work. The Stock Exchange's 'Model Code for Securities Transactions by Directors of Listed Companies' forbids directors to deal in the two

Business and religion are more in tune in the United States. This hymn is sung by the Rev. Al and his Prayer Family together with their congregation in Fresno in California.

God is like Coca-Cola – He's the real thing.
God is like Pan Am – He makes the going great.
God is like General Electric – He lights your path.
God is like Bayer Aspirin – He works wonders.
God is like Hallmark Cards – He cares enough to send the very best.
God is like Tide – He gets the stains out that others leave behind.
God is like VO5 Hair Spray – He holds through all kinds of weather.
God is like Dial Soap – Aren't you glad you know Him? Don't you wish everybody did?
God is like Sears – He has everything.
God is like Alka-Seltzer – Try Him, you'll like Him.
God is like Scotch Tape – You can't see Him but you know He's there.

months before the announcements of either the interim or full results, except in exceptional circumstances. Nor can they deal prior to the announcement of price-sensitive information. They are also supposed to restrain themselves from dealing on 'considerations of a short-term nature.'

The dealings of directors can be a useful guide to the financial health of a company. Although such deals are only one piece of the overall jigsaw, it is hard to imagine a director plunging his own hard-earned cash into the shares if the business is about to go down the plughole. Similarly, he is unlikely to dump his entire holding if the company's future looks glittering. There may be other factors, of course. Asking directors why they have sold shares can prove extremely interesting. It is rare for one to tell you that prospects for the company are looking less rosy. On the contrary, it is far more likely that he will claim he needs the money for a swimming pool, or the kids' school fees or a new conservatory or perhaps a rainy day brewing up on the horizon.

Directors have to inform their company secretaries of their dealings within five working days, detailing the number of shares and the price paid or received. The company must then notify the Stock Exchange immediately. Although everyone in the City may see the announcement of what has transpired on the various news services there, it is surprisingly hard for we mortals outside the glittering Square Mile to find out what is going on. The *Financial Times* used to devote quite a bit of space to directors' dealings. Now they carry no more than five or six deals in a week. The chances of a company you are interested in being included are rare.

However, other sources of information on directors' share purchases and sales have sprung up, such as the magazine *The Inside Track* from Directus (031–220 0468). It seems potty that investors should not know what their directors are doing with their own shares. Their dealings may be the first indication that something is going wrong, or right, with the business.

I do not know whether company directors as a breed have memories worse than the national average, but an extraordinary number seem to forget to notify their companies or the Stock Exchange about what they have done, suddenly remembering again months later. Surprise, surprise, by the time the outside world knows of their transaction, the reason behind it is also crystal clear. The Stock Exchange has claimed that as many as 15% of all announcements from public companies in this area are deficient in some respect. This figure doesn't only include tiny little out of the way businesses, but some of the top firms in the land. I can't think of many instances, however, of the Companies Act provisions being invoked so that directors who do have such memory lapses are fined or imprisoned. The maximum term is two years. If only one or two examples were made of directors who had reported share transactions a year late, I am sure that the others would enrol for memory-improving courses straight away and that problem would clear up in no time at all.

I still remember the case of one company chairman who decided to give every last one of his shares to his girlfriend as a gift. She decided to sell them immediately but, not being a member of his family, did not need to make a declaration of the fact to the company. This act of selfless generosity looked a little less altruistic in the light of his subsequent resignation and the sharp downturn in the company's profits. The chap was soon in the dock, trying to explain the sequence of events and subsequently became the first insider dealer to be imprisoned in this country. Directors don't always get away with blue murder. It just seems like it at times.

Should, heaven forbid, there ever be an unwelcome takeover bid for one of your companies, you would expect your directors to make a Herculean effort to fight off the bid or, if necessary, to ensure that the highest possible price is paid by the predator. There is, unfortunately, a great deal of evidence that at this most crucial of times, the interests of shareholders and directors do not always coincide.

For a start, the directors' jobs could be on the line, particularly if the bidding company is accusing existing management of incompetence and of having been responsible for the failure of the company to achieve its true potential. The need to protect their own position could become paramount

[87]

> Although there is no indication that anyone has tried it, it has been suggested that there is a perfect way for companies to see off possible bidders, with none of the usual exorbitant costs associated with a full-blown defence.
>
> If you believe another company to be considering a bid, send them some vital information about your firm by registered mail. Being in possession of inside information about your business will make it illegal for the aggressor to buy your shares!

in the board's minds, especially if they realise that their own limitations make the finding of alternative employment somewhat unlikely, unless they fancy becoming dustmen or lavatory cleaners.

If it looks possible that the bid will succeed, the directors may attempt to make sure that they do as well out of it as possible. Bids seldom come entirely out of the blue and a period of speculation about a possible takeover could give them the chance to write themselves new, lucrative service contracts and to grant themselves a few extra options. If a director's service contract has almost five years to run, anyone kicking that chap out on his ear is going to have to pay him five years' salary all in one go, a pretty sharp disincentive to a bidder, particularly if the majority of the board have similar contracts. Even if the contract hasn't been granted particularly recently, the sums of money involved can be so great as to affect the plans of the bidder.

In 1986, Ratners took over H Samuel, making them the biggest force in the UK jewellery market. Anthony Edgar had run that, and although he became group chairman of the entire group, he left after just four months. It cost Ratners £535,000 to buy out the remaining four years of his service contract.

The amount of outstanding options may also be an important factor. A bid will usually increase the share price substantially, making directors' options suddenly far more valuable. If the bid goes ahead, they could make a lot of money. If the bid fails and the price has a relapse, all that extra cash might never materialise. What a dilemma.

The Takeover Panel took a dim view of the goings on at textile group, John Crowther, early in 1988. In March the chairman, Trevor Barker, was granted options on 93,750 shares at 128p each. The finance director David Suddens, was granted options on 234,375 shares, also at 128p. Two days later, Coloroll made a takeover bid for the company. Although a rival offer materialised, Coloroll eventually won control. The profit on both sets of options would have been around £200,000. There were also other options already outstanding. The tough old Takeover panel, well known for its ability to point out that the stable door really should have been locked but as the horse has already bolted there is really little that can be done about it, looked into the matter and decided that, although it really should have been consulted, the Takeover Code had not been breached.

Salary increases granted on the same day as the options also helped boost the total compensation package. The chairman's salary had been £60,000 less than six months earlier. By the time the bid came, it was £115,000. It was announced by Coloroll that, if its bid succeeded, the chairman of Crowthers was to receive £482,400, the deputy chairman £360,850 and the finance director £132,390. All three would cease to be board members. In response to press criticism, the chairman of Coloroll, John Ashcroft, pointed out that the payments were only a reflection of the compensation necessary to buy out the remainder of the directors' three-year service contracts. And, as he told one journalist, 'one man's definition of excessive is another's derisory sum.' Quite so. R.I.P. Coloroll.

The other element of the compensation package in the

Crowther takeover was that the deputy chairman was also able to buy his company Mercedes 560 SEL for just a pound, while the finance director's Volvo 760 GLT was sold to him for the same sum. This prompted one leading public relations chap to announce that he would be willing to bid as much as five pounds for the Mercedes!

> Let it not be thought that stockbrokers are completely without a sense of humour, even if it is derived from Monty Python. Contained in a stock market report was this comment: 'Steetley gained 11p to 349p as the details of the Spanish deal sank in while Metal Box, which also announced a buy in Spain this week, fell back a couple of pence to 235p. "Nobody expected the Spanish acquisition," was the comment of a wag at Warburgs.'

When Rowntree was taken over by Nestlé at £10.75 cash per share, some directors of the company were able to exercise options which had been granted at prices as low as £1.58! At the beginning of 1988, ten board members had options over 533,212 shares. The vast majority were exercisable at £5.70 which, prior to the bid when the shares languished below £5, must have looked a very unattractive prospect. Not so a few months later when there was a profit of £5.05 to be had on each. 42 senior executives of the company around the world were granted options over 760,000 in July 1987 at £5.70. The total profit on those, within less than a year, was nearly four million pounds.

Shareholders ought to bear in mind clause 11 of the Takeover Code. 'Directors of an offeror or an offeree company shall always, in advising their shareholders, act only in their capacity as directors and not have regard to their personal or family shareholding or their personal relationships with the company. It is the shareholders' interests taken as a whole, together with those of employees and creditors, which should be considered.'

As I mentioned earlier, it is frequently difficult to find out exactly how well directors are doing out of your company. Yet you should always remember that no matter how good the various members of the board are, the more they get paid, the less money there is in the coffers for other more trivial things such as reinvestment, research and development and paying the shareholders. Directors' pay always seems to go up. If there is another downturn in corporate profits, it seems about as likely that their remuneration will turn downwards as it does that pigs will be granted the right to use the runway at Heathrow.

It is perhaps time that shareholders started taking a greater interest in the board's interests in their company. Although the information given on the matter in Annual Reports is woefully inadequate, it is possible for shareholders to learn a great deal more. Directors' service contracts of more than a year's duration have to be made available for inspection by shareholders without charge. And, as the Annual Report will point out, from the date of its posting until the AGM anybody can look at them. At the AGM itself, there is an obligation to allow anyone to look at them from at least a quarter of an hour in advance of the meeting until it is over. The Register of Directors' Interests must also be made similarly available for inspection at the AGM.

Occasionally, but just occasionally, we are able to glimpse not only the ordinary remuneration of those at the top, but also those little extras that go to make life a bit more bearable. When Britoil was taken over by BP, the retiring chairman, Sir Philip Shelbourne, was retained as a consultant, working for the company three days each month.

Formerly on £138,000, Sir Philip's post-acquisition remuneration package was £24,000 a year towards lunch expenses, use of a car with driver, travel and hotel expenses, private health cover, £40,000 a year in lieu of office facilities and, last but by no means least, four tickets for each season at Covent Garden Opera House and four tickets for the Centre Court at Wimbledon on the day of the men's finals!

The directors have it in their power to spread a fair bit of shareholders' cash around without asking the views of those shareholders. A great deal is given by the corporate sector each year to various charities. The largest 200 quoted companies are estimated to donate something over £60 million each year. This seems fair enough. It might be nice if more companies followed the example of an American firm, Berkshire Hathaway, which tells shareholders the maximum it plans to donate, and then lets them indicate to which particular charity they would like their portion to go. This sort of democracy is sadly alien to British companies.

Less acceptable is the assumption that shareholders are happy to see their money donated to the Conservative Party. Without funding from British companies, the Tories' finances would be in a perilous state. It is a peculiar political system where one of the two main parties is funded by the unions and the other by the employers, but we would appear to be stuck with it for the foreseeable future. It seems even more peculiar, however, that companies are allowed to hand over considerable sums for political purposes without asking permission first. The sum of £2m to £3m a year does not sound an enormous amount when set against total charitable donations, but individual companies' donations to the party can be very substantial.

Although one or two firms donate to the centre parties, only one has recently helped with Labour Party funds. In

1988, the amusement hall operator Singleton Holdings contributed £1,000, their first company donation since the
design group Aidcom was taken over. It had balloted its
workers on their preferences and donated accordingly.

The vast majority of political donations, therefore, are to
the Conservative Party or related bodies. Taylor Woodrow,
for instance, gave £150,000 to Conservative party funds in
1990. Other substantial donors are United Biscuits,
Trusthouse Forte, Hanson, Allied Lyons, P & O and the
Rank Organisation. Yet very few firms ask shareholders'
permission. Of the larger groups, only Marks & Spencer,
Rank Organisation and some of the investment trusts do
so. The new management of B&C creditably took the
opportunity of the company's 1988 AGM to confirm that
shareholders did wish to continue to donate to Conservative funds. The motion was overwhelmingly carried but
it was not long before the company had other problems on
its plate.

The matter of political donations is frequently raised at
AGMs and the general attitude of the chairmen is that the
Conservatives have brought about such a substantial
change in the business climate in Britain that shareholders
should be only too happy to see their money used in this
way. The majority may well agree. But the question should
surely be put to the vote, not left to the whim of the
directors, whose knighthoods may owe something to the
generosity of their shareholders' money.

Trade unions have to hold a ballot on their political fund
every ten years. Why should companies not be forced to
ballot their shareholders in a similar manner?

Whose company is it anyway?

The illustrious Lord Denning must have seen his fair
share of directors come before him in his time. Let me end
this chapter with his words.

[93]

'Directors are not liable for anything, for only the company is a legal entity. The shareholders have no real voice. Companies are run by directors who are self-perpetuating and self-elected and who run their company accountable to no-one except to an annual meeting of shareholders which very few, if any, ever attend. They are only accountable by reason of these glossy annual reports giving a most persuasive air to what they have been doing.

The private investor has no say at all, and no control.'

Perhaps it is about time we tried winning back a little ground.

6

'Dear Shareholder . . .'

Isn't it extraordinary how perfectly ordinary people who usually have no difficulty in speaking perfectly ordinary English go to pieces and lapse into gobbledegook when they have to speak to investors. I have grumbled about the complexity and near incomprehensibility of financial documentation for years. I am inclined to believe practically every company executive I have ever discussed this matter with when, to a man, and a woman, they point the finger in one direction – at the lawyers. They claim that whenever they try, as ordinary human beings, to attempt to couch something in plain English, the lawyers claim it can't be done like that without the risk of incurring the biggest lawsuit this side of the Atlantic. By the time the 'heretofores' and 'notwithstandings' have been slotted into place, the document is ten times the size it was to begin with. As a result the only people able to understand it are those fortunate enough to have law degrees.

Many investors at whom such documents are aimed take one look at their thickness and throw them straight into the waste paper bin, assuming they have the constitution of a shot-putter. At the top of each is usually an insulting instruction along the lines of: 'This document is important and requires your immediate attention. When considering what action you should take you are recommended to seek your own personal financial advice from your stockbroker, bank manager, solicitor, accountant or other professional adviser.' In other words: 'You are just a private investor, mate and so are far, far, beneath us. This document is written in big boy's language and there isn't a cat's chance in hell that you will have the slightest idea what it is all about. Throw it in the bin and you risk missing out on something important. Go to your financial adviser instead and he will be able to earn some nice fat fees from you for converting the thing back into English.'

You only need to hold shares in one company to realise that I am not exaggerating. Practically every document that comes through the letterbox is written in another language entirely, and one only vaguely related to English. This is unfortunately every bit as true of the privatised companies as of all the others, despite the importance of making sure that new shareholders understand what is going on. Notices informing investors that the second or third calls on their shares are due have been among the most complex documents I have ever encountered, while the British Gas dividend warrants, which had four separate sections, were extremely confusing even to someone who is well used to the look of dividend cheques. It is hardly any wonder that 50,000 investors had still not cashed their October 1987 cheques after four months; they probably didn't realise what they were, even though the outstanding amount in February 1988 was as much as a million pounds.

The full British Gas prospectus ran to a massive 80 pages although there was also a simplified version produced. Both versions, however, included the longest clause I have

The Japanese are comic mad. Everyone, but everyone, in Japan seems to read them. But the *Mangas*, as they are known, are very different from our Beano and Dandy. There are Mills & Boon type comics, Western comics, food comics and pornographic comics. So keen are the Japanese on them, that the *mangas* are seen as an excellent way of educating the populace about matters that might be considered too boring in ordinary book form.

Finance is one such area, with Japan's Economic Planning Agency issuing a comic version of its annual white paper on the economy. One *Manga* in this field, Hisaichi Ishii's Econocomics, aims to teach his countrymen what's what.

For some reason, one or two pages have English translations, showing that Japanese have more of a sense of humour than they are sometimes credited with.

Two characters are talking at a Securities House.

A: Ha ha ha ha. We're making a killing. With everyone playing the stock market, all the securities firms are showing twodigit profit growth.
B: But if we make too much money, people will start demanding lower commissions and liberalization of the market like they did in America.
A: We can't let that happen. We've got to show some kind of loss.
B: That's no problem boss. All we have to do is set up a separate company and have it play the stock market. Then we'll lose money.

The semiconductor industry also features. A group of American businessmen are standing round grumbling: 'Japan has to stop dumping and import more American semiconductors,' says one. They then all start smashing up Japanese semiconductors with little hammers.

The Japanese businessmen are similarly indignant. 'They might call it neo-nationalism, but let's get our spirits up by smashing American semiconductors.' But they are thwarted in their attempts when they open up the crates. 'They're all defective. They're already broken,' they wail.

THE SHAREHOLDER

come across in any financial document. A masterpiece of lawyerese it has, in case you are not inclined to count them for yourself, 180 words. Clause (i) is one of thirteen clauses, all beginning 'By completing and delivering an application form, you: – ' This one read: 'Authorise the relevant receiving bank and the Custodian Bank to send a letter of acceptance for the number of Ordinary Shares for which your application is accepted and/or a cheque for any money returnable by post at your risk to the address of the person (or the first-named person) named in the application form and to procure that your name (and the name(s) of any other joint applicant(s)) is placed on the register of holders of interim rights in respect of such Ordinary Shares the entitlement to which has not been effectively renounced and thereafter to procure that your name (and the names(s) of any other joint applicant(s)) is placed on the register of members of the Company in respect of such Ordinary Shares the entitlement to which is evidenced by Interim Certificates and the right to which has not been effectively transferred: and in these terms and conditions references to rights being effectively renounced mean the renouncee(s) being registered by a receiving bank in relation to such rights.'

If you are at this moment saying to yourself: 'What is wrong with that? Seems perfectly clear to me' then I have no wish ever to meet you. We wouldn't get on.

Mercifully, it seems that the lawyers working on the privatisation issues realised just how daft that particular clause was, helped in that understanding no doubt when the sentence won a Golden Bull award from the Plain English campaigners. By the time the British Petroleum prospectus was released, the clause ran to a mere 106 words. Some improvement!

Fortunately some companies are aware of the seriousness of the problem. Writing in *The Shareholder* magazine, the company secretary of British Gas said: 'Too many of the standard pieces of paper which shareholders receive – proxy forms, dividend warrants, reminders about uncashed dividends and Annual Reports all seem to be written by and for lawyers and accountants. This was all very well in the days when shareholding was a matter for a select few, and the initiated were talking to their fellow initiates. The assumption seems to have been that shareholders were either professional investors, or were wealthy enough to have stockbrokers and accountants to look after their affairs for them. This does not apply to Sid.' Nice though it is to know that the problem is recognised, it seems to be taking an awfully long time for companies to remedy it.

Not everything that drops onto shareholders' doormats is pure gobbledegook. Whole sections of companies' Annual Reports are in fact comprehensible to the layman. The most widely read section for this very reason is the Chairman's Statement. Perhaps because so many chairmen have only the vaguest idea of what all the figures mean themselves, they tend to write in English that we can all

---

The Annual Report sent out in 1988 by Barclays Bank had the usual group photograph of the company's senior management, arranged conveniently at one end of a beautiful table.

Somewhat odd, though, was the rather detached appearance of the deputy chairman of Barclays de Zoete Wedd, Lord Camoys. With his skin a completely different complexion from the others and some strange lines around his torso, the untrained eye might almost have thought that his picture was pasted in afterwards. Or did the other directors pose with a cardboard cutout?

[100]

understand. Whether we should believe a word they say is another matter of course. Chairmen have to have many of the skills of the successful politician and it would be wise of shareholders to remember, as they read the account of how their company has been managed over the past year, that this is the only section of the document whose contents are not covered by statute or by Stock Exchange regulations.

Occasionally, but just occasionally, a chairman is frank enough for shareholders to believe implicitly everything they are being told. Unfortunately, the very few examples of this I have so far encountered have all come from the other side of the Atlantic. Take the electronics group Teradyne. Its vice-president in charge of corporate relations, Frederick T. Van Veen, felt that he had always wanted to write a truly candid report. He got his wish.

'Most of Teradyne's 26 years have been very good, and many of them have been spectacular. A small number – five to be exact – have been bad, if you define bad as meaning a year of no growth. 1986 was definitely one of the bad ones.

'. . . A Profit and Loss Statement with no Profit is lamentable, but it is certainly survivable. Overall, our sales were down by about 9%, which doesn't sound so bad when you say it fast.

'. . . What we thought was an insatiable demand for personal computers was satiable as it turned out.

'. . . The language in Japan is a big problem. In Europe, an American can at least read street signs . . . in Japan it's all Greek, so to speak.'

That refreshing style is all too rare in the Annual Reports of UK companies. It is not, however, completely absent, particularly when chairmen use it as the occasion to get rid of a few bees from their bonnets. Take Thomas Kenny, chairman of Ruberoid. Here are a few extracts from the 1987 Annual Report.

'We have done it. My aim of but a few years ago has been achieved. We have made our first £10 million of operating profit in 1987. This is the twelfth year of continuous profit growth. Thank you John Roberts and your team. It is a great credit to you and to them. Were it not for two black sheep, one in particular, the results would have been better. In a Group of our size it is almost inevitable that one or other subsidiary will be out of line from time to time.

'To be more specific. Pre-tax profits of £10,191,000 are 12% ahead of 1986 and that is before extraordinary realised gains of £1,289,000. So many accounts nowadays are spattered with exceptional and extraordinary items which is generally a euphemism for losses. With us this year it means profit.

'Group sales at £145 million are 5% ahead of 1986. Almost one half of our sales were outside the UK.

'The tax man joins the party and hopes to collect over £3 million.

'. . . I have not seen the Finance Bill 1988 due for publication on 14 April. My knowledge is limited to press reports. If I read it aright there is nothing significant in our favour but nationally it seems good. So why blot it with absurd and petty proposals?

'An imaginative civil servant suggests something new – an increased tax on tobacco and beer! Another bonehead goes further. You can now only spend a total of £10 tax deductible on entertaining overseas customers. The Treasury think that our overseas customers with substantial orders in their pockets come to the UK on a London bus ticket. 600 Members of Parliament are going to debate the matter.

'. . . It is rumoured that the next Companies Act will make provision for statutory accounts to be divided between those that are understandable and those that are not. Despite the constraints on the preparation of accounts we try to make ours as simple as possible.

'Next year we will have a full year's contributions from our interest in Nebiprofa and eight months' contribution from the additional shares in Norwich Corrugated Board. So, if you wish to anticipate good profits in 1988, I will not try to dissuade you. The year has started well.'

The previous Report included the following: '1986, for Ruberoid, was a great year. Profits up: dividend up; cash up and net assets up from £23 million to £29 million.

'This is our eleventh year of profit improvement. Not all companies can make that boast. I enjoy making it and so does our management team. If you need proof of the merit of decentralised management and a tiny head office structure we can give it to you.

'. . . The taxman joins the party and takes 37.6% of our profits costing £3,434,000. The media headlines intrigue me. "Chancellor gives away . . ." Rubbish, he can only give away what we have given him already.'

However, shareholders were perhaps not quite so enthusiastic about the performance of Ruberoid's board for, in mid-1988, they accepted the terms of a takeover offer.

James Sherwood, chairman of Sea Containers, is another who has used the Annual Report to grind an axe or two. A subsidiary of his company is Sealink and, in his 1985 Annual Report, he wrote about the Channel Tunnel project: 'The bid turned out to be a political farce. A group of ten construction companies, five on each side of the Channel, was given the award to build a rail-shuttle system at enormous cost, offering an obsolete transport method with little time savings over the ferries. Our bid was rejected by President Mitterrand because we didn't have French partners and his acceptance would be construed as "selling out to the English" at a time of French national elections . . . Mitterrand's party lost anyway.'

Mining companies in the distant reaches of Australia and Canada can be amongst the riskiest investments of all.

One stockbrokers' circular gave the following advice to clients. 'Given that the shares are fully paid, the downside risk is only 100 per cent.'

My favourite chairman's statement of all comes from the interim report of United Bancorporation Alaska, Inc, dated June 30th 1987. John T. Shiveley, chairman of the board, seems to have decided that there is no point at all in beating about the bush. It seems a shame to précis this at all. This is his statement in its entirety.

'The good news is that I am able to write my second letter to the Shareholders. The bad news is we lost $83.7 million in the first six months of the year. You undoubtedly thought that things couldn't get worse and that nobody could lose that amount of money in such a short period of time. One excuse is that I am new to the banking business and, having read about the major losses being incurred by the large money centre banks, I became confused. I realise that $83.7 million is a pittance compared to the billions of dollars the big boys are losing, but we all have to start somewhere.

'Seriously, two extremely critical events for the Company occurred during the second quarter. The first event occurred on June 23, 1987 when the Company entered into an agreement to merge with Alaska Mutual Bancorporation (AMB), another Alaska chartered bank holding company. As part of a plan of restructuring, the FDIC (Federal Deposit Insurance Corporation) will raise $65 million for AMB, which will be the survivor of a merger between UBAI and AMB. For each share you currently own of UBAI stock, you will receive .05 shares in the merged company and you will have the right to purchase additional shares in order to retain a proportionate interest in the merged company. If you do not purchase additional shares, your ownership interest will be substantially diluted. If the plan of restructuring is successfuly implemented, UBA and Alaska Mutual Bank will not be closed by the regulators. In mid-September, if our current schedule holds, you should be receiving a long and boring joint proxy statement and prospectus that will explain the whole transaction. As you attempt to read the proxy statement, keep in mind that its main purpose is to provide attorneys an opportunity to generate hundreds of billable hours. If we did not provide this kind of make-work project for people in the legal profession, they might have to go out and find real jobs. I do recommend that you read the proxy statement as it contains important information on the proposed merger.

'The second significant event for the Company involved a hard look at the Company's financial situation. Evaluations to estimate current values of real estate collateral for loans and other real estate owned were done throughout 1986 by the Company. When I came on as the new Chairman of the Board and Chief Executive Officer of the Company earlier this year, several of the previous assumptions and estimates of underlying real estate values had changed considerably since the end of 1986. The recession in Alaska has deepened during 1987 and interest rates have increased, which have produced negative influences on the real estate market.

'Based on analyses completed using the revised assumptions and estimates, the Company has increased its allowance for loan losses to $74.6 million or 27.69% of loans at June 30, 1987. As a result of the increase in the allowance and a substantial write-down of other real estate owned, UBAI lost $83.7 million during the first half of 1987. This loss created a deficit in Shareholders' equity of $77.6 million.

'I personally have taken a very conservative view of the Alaskan real estate market. In the early 1980s, however, the majority of the people in the state felt that the real estate development boom would last indefinitely. Unfortunately, the boom came to a crashing halt.

Since the 1920s, the New York Stock Exchange has restricted the number of its seats to 1,366.

The fixed supply led to prices being boosted sharply in the great bull market of the 1980s. When one changed hands for $1.1 million in the summer of 1987, the more cautious pointed out that the last time those sort of prices was seen was in 1929.

Just months later, the market crashed. Perhaps an index of these seat prices should be constructed, so that we are given an early warning signal next time.

'Many observers have blamed the crash of the Alaskan economy on the decline in oil prices and oil industry activity. The problems faced by the energy industry certainly contributed to Alaska's current economic problems.

However, I believe a more serious problem for the banking industry here is that there is a substantial over-supply of commercial and residential real estate. In more simple terms, Alaska banks were financing the building of condos, houses and shopping centres for the people who were building condos, houses and shopping centres. When the building stopped and other sectors of the economy began to disintegrate, people working in the construction industry and other ailing businesses began to leave and now we don't need all those condos, houses and shopping centres. Although blowing up tankers in the Gulf of Oman may help bring stability to the U.S. oil industry, I believe that Alaska needs more than just an increase in oil prices to solve its economic woes.

'The plan that has been formulated by UBAI, AMB and Hallwood should address the financial problems of UBAI and AMB and, assuming consummation, create a financially stable resulting entity.

'As I have been conveying little but bad news to you since I began this job in April, you may be pleased to hear that, as a condition of contributing $295 million, the FDIC requires senior management of both UBAI and AMB to leave at the close of the transaction. With a little luck, the new CEO of the merged company should be able to report more encouraging news to you than I have been able to.'

That's telling 'em, John! You will not be surprised to learn that the original copy of this statement now has pride of place on my office noticeboard.

Warren Buffett is considered to be one of America's shrewdest investors. He has run Berkshire Hathaway, a holding company with subsidiaries operating in diverse business areas, for nearly a quarter of a century. Over that time, the shares have risen from $12 each to $3,400 and

Berkshire's Annual Reports have become widely sought after. There are no photographs or gimmicks, just Buffett's sheer common sense and his homespun lessons in investment. This is from the 1987 Report.

'Gypsy Rose Lee announced on one of her later birthdays: "I have everything I had last year; it's just that it's all two inches lower." During 1987 almost all of our businesses aged in a more upbeat way. There's not a lot new to report about these businesses – and that's good, not bad. Severe change and exceptional returns usually don't mix. Most investors, of course, behave as if just the opposite were true. They usually confer the highest price-earnings ratios on exotic-sounding businesses that hold out the promise of feverish change. That prospect lets investors fantasize about future profitability rather than face today's business realities. For such investor-dreamers, any blind date is preferable to one with the girl next door, no matter how desirable she may be.'

Later on he advises that: 'In my opinion, investment success will not be produced by arcane formulae, computer programs or signals flashed by the price behaviour of stocks and markets. Rather an investor will succeed by coupling good business judgment with an ability to insulate his thoughts and behaviour from the super-contagious emotions that swirl about the marketplace . . . I let our marketable equities tell us by their operating results – not by their daily, or even yearly, price quotations – whether our investments are successful. The market may ignore business success for a while, but eventually it will confirm it. Delayed recognition can be an advantage: It may give us the chance to buy more of a good thing at a bargain price.'
Commenting upon the extraordinary behaviour of the

> The October 1987 Crash showed up the terrible problems of liquidity in many of the shares that make up the market. It brought a totally new category of shares into common parlance, the Night-Owl Stocks.
>
> These are so-called because, if someone tries to sell any of them, the cry goes up: 'Twit! To who?'

markets in October 1987, Buffett, with Olympian disdain, says: 'Many commentators have drawn an incorrect conclusion upon observing recent events: They are fond of saying that the small investor has no chance in a market now dominated by the erratic behaviour of the big boys. This conclusion is dead wrong: such markets are ideal for an investor – small or large – so long as he sticks to his investment knitting. Volatility caused by money managers who speculate irrationally with huge sums will offer the true investor more chances to make intelligent investment moves. He can be hurt by such volatility only if he is forced, by either financial or psychological pressures, to sell at untoward times.'

Buffett is not particularly keen on short-term investors. He has even proposed that a capital gains tax be brought in at a rate of 100% on anything sold within a year of purchase. In these days when companies and securities houses are building bright, glitzy, monuments to their greatness and spending hundreds of thousands of pounds on fitting out their offices, it is interesting to note that Berkshire Hathaway has just seven employees in its headquarters. They are situated in a corner of one floor in an Omaha office block. It is fairly peaceful there too. One of America's greatest investors refuses to install any machines there showing up-to-date share prices.

Buffet's Reports are priceless in themselves. He is, heaven forbid, not even above trying to make his shareholders laugh. Discussing the chairman of one of Berkshire's subsidiaries, Nebraska Furniture Mart, Buffett goes so far as to mention a lady's age. He actually tells us that Mrs B, as Rose Blumkin is known, is 94. She started her business over 50 years ago with 500 dollars. It is now the biggest home furnishings store in the United States. 'Mrs B continues to work seven days a week at the job from the opening of each business day until the close. She buys, she sells, she manages – and she runs rings around the competition. It's clear to me that she's gathering speed and may well reach her full potential in another five or ten years. Therefore, I've persuaded the Board to scrap our mandatory-retirement-at-a-hundred policy. (And it's about time: with every passing year, this policy has seemed sillier to me.)'

Anyone believing that private investors are at a disadvantage to the institutions, or that investment is boring, should read, re-read and then re-read again some of Buffett's Annual Reports. He speaks with a disarming frankness at times, such as in his 1986 Report.

'We bought a corporate jet last year. What you have heard about such planes is true: they are very expensive and a luxury in situations like ours where little travel to out-of-the-way places is required. And planes not only cost a lot to operate, they cost a lot just to look at. Pre-tax, cost of capital plus depreciation on a new $15 million plane probably runs $3 million annually. On our own plane, bought for $850,000 used, such costs run close to $200,000 annually.

'Cognizant of such figures, your Chairman, unfortunately, has in the past made a number of rather intemperate remarks about corporate jets. Accordingly, prior to our purchase, I was forced into my Galileo mode. I promptly experienced the necessary "counter-revelation" and travel is now considerably easier – and considerably costlier – than in the past. Whether Berkshire will get its money's worth from the plane is an open question, but I will work at achieving some business triumph that I can (no matter how dubiously) attribute to it. I'm afraid Ben Franklin had my number. Said he: "So convenient a thing it is to be a reasonable creature, since it enables one to find or make a reason for everything one has a mind to do."'

Some British company chairmen aren't above a little levity and straight talking, particularly if the companies really are 'theirs' to a large degree. However, the best examples I can find come not from their statements in the Annual Reports, but from interviews in the press. My two favourite chairmen in this area are Gerald Ratner and Alan Sugar. Ratner is refreshingly frank about the best way to sell jewellery. In a profile in the *Financial Times* he stressed the importance of displaying jewellery properly: 'We put coloured stone ear-rings at an angle so that the light shines on them and they sparkle.'

He was asked how the company could sell a lead crystal sherry decanter with six matching, egg-cup shaped glasses on a silver plated tray for just £14.99. His cousin Victor replied: 'Buying.' Gerald's answer was: 'Because it's crap.'

Still, he seems to offer customers jewellery at affordable prices. He makes no bones about the future value of what he sells, claiming that: 'Diamonds are a very bad investment – especially ours.'

Alan Sugar has had a fairly stormy relationship with the City over the years. He appears not to be over-enamoured of the young analysts who have consistently poo-pooed prospects for his company, Amstrad, even though it has exceeded their expectations in practically every year of trading. As his half-holding in the company is worth around half a billion pounds, Sugar can afford to let his temper show from time to time. He once revealed that he knew so little of Cityspeak in his early days, that, when asked about his PE by a merchant banker, he claimed to do ten press-ups a day.

He was furious about the recent sale of the Ferguson television company to the French, despite his wish to buy it, calling it a 'dead diabolical liberty.' His rivals have also come in for a fair amount of stick. When Olivetti produced a rival for the Amstrad Personal Computer, Sugar's response was to call it 'a pregnant calculator.'

As far as he is concerned, though, the customer is king, an un-British attitude surely responsible for much of his company's success. When Amstrad's personal computer was first launched, there was an extraordinary whispering campaign in the City, spread further by one national Sunday newspaper, hinting at problems with the machine. Much of this revolved around the possibility of it overheating because there was no fan in it. Sugar insisted there was no possibility of overheating and that no fan was necessary, but soon capitulated. All new machines had fans installed. Sugar said: 'If it's the difference between people buying the machine or not, I'll stick a bloody fan in it. And if they say they want bright pink spots on it, I'll do that too. What is the use of me banging my head against a brick wall and saying "You don't need the damn fan, sunshine?"'

At one time, there was widespread speculation that Amstrad was going to manufacture car phones. To still this, Sugar claimed that he would only do that when pigs fly. One analyst, more appreciative of Sugar's abilities than most, claimed that this might not mean the great man did not intend plunging into the car phone market. On the contrary, it could mean that not only did he intend making them, but he also intended manufacturing flying pigs as

---

Darryl Gammill, a Denver investment adviser, believes that music is the key to picking shares. Using a computer, he converts share price charts into orchestrated pieces. 'If the stock sounds very low,' says Gammill, 'when it goes BOOM, BOOM, BOOM – that's a buy signal. If people will just relax and listen to the music, the harmonics will tell you where the stock is going.'

He turned IBM's share chart into two difference pieces: 'Rhapsody in Big Blue,' was the more classical of the two. 'Decisions, decisions,' was aimed at the soft-rock fans.

Sounds barmy? The Book-of-the-Month Club didn't think so. They offered a cassette of Mr Gammill's tunes in their catalogue.

---

well. For the life of him, though, he could not see where the demand for them was going to come from!

I find it rather refreshing when company representatives are able to come out from behind their grey cloaks and speak out frankly and openly. It is a shame that it happens so rarely. Perhaps directors are terrified of tempting fate, believing that if they crow too much when times are good, their words will be thrown back at them when things are a little less rosy. They should be braver. Whatever their peers may think, I am sure the majority of shareholders would prefer it. After all, English is our first language, not legalese or accountancyese.

This hatred of speaking what is really in their minds means that when reading through the majority of chairmen's statements, investors should try to look at what is concealed between the lines, as well as on them. I am indebted to that most personable of Wall Street gurus, Bob Stovall, who sent me the following examples of statements from chief executives' letters to shareholders, together with Bob's explanations of what he reckons they really mean.

[113]

The first is from Eastern Airlines. The rest he refuses to divulge.

'The quarter's earnings contained a substantial contribution from a settlement arising from the involuntary termination of operating equipment.' *If the plane hadn't crashed we would have been in the red. Fortunately no-one was killed. The insurance company paid off more than the value we had depreciated it to.*

'Divestiture of this division will allow management to concentrate on the company's historic business, while allowing a greater consumer identity with those traditional lines.' *We never should have bought that disaster, and it took us five years to come up with a buyer. Now we can go back to our basic business.*

'Management has been fortunate in having the opportunity to acquire considerable experience in this and allied fields of endeavour.' *We've made a lot of collective mistakes in our time – not only at this company, but a lot of other places too.*

'It would be less than totally honest to say that we are proud of the results so far this year.' *The second best policy is dishonesty – but we can't possibly hide this disaster.*

'Earnings reached 53 cents a share which, in light of your company's long historical record, should be considered reasonably acceptable.' *That's what we earned 10 years ago.*

'Those results were somewhat below the projections that management had announced publicly during the quarter.' *We guessed wrong on this one.*

'Various accounting adjustments contributed the bulk of reported earnings during the quarter. However, these are not expected to be a significant factor in future quarters.' *We pay big fees to a creative accounting firm. And if they don't continue to come up with ploys like this, we'll find another even more creative firm.*

'Your management is never satisfied with earnings merely being acceptable, although in light of prevailing economic conditions these results would certainly be reasonable.' *At least we didn't have to cut the dividend.*

'Regarding the resignation of the president during the quarter, management has enthusiastically asked him to continue to serve the company in an advisory capacity.' *If we sacked him outright he might talk to the press.*

'Management has taken significant steps to ensure the long-term continuity of the present team of professional managers.' *The chairman of the board and the largest stockholder has just become a grandfather.*

'We thank the stockholders for the trust they have placed in management and promise that our commitment to growth and excellence remains firmly intact.' *Stockholder attempts to throw out management are difficult when that same management owns over half the stock.*

'We thank the stockholders for the trust they have placed in management by approving the present salary 10-year contracts for senior officers and directors of the company, to be valid regardless of changing circumstances.' *Management owns less than half the stock – but we got our 'golden parachutes' through anyway.*

7

Brushing up that Dull Old Image

There are good managements and bad managements. Unfortunately the one thing many bad managers are good at is giving the impression that they are good managers. How can we poor, humble, private investors avoid being taken in by them? After all, unlike the institutions, we rarely get a chance to meet them or to glimpse the way they operate. All we have to go on are what they show us and it is all too easy to be impressed by the incredible vitality and activity apparently displayed by so many managers. They are helped by an often sycophantic press, always on the lookout for a businessman vain enough to provide enough material to fill a quarter of a page or more.

It is interesting to read the views of Warren Buffett on this: 'Experience indicates that the best business returns are usually achieved by companies that are doing something quite similar today to what they were doing five or ten years ago. That is no argument for managerial complacency. Businesses always have opportunities to improve service, product lines, manufacturing techniques, and the like, and obviously these opportunities should be seized. But a business that constantly encounters major change also encounters many chances for major error. Furthermore, economic terrain that is forever shifting violently is ground on which it is difficult to build a fortress-like business franchise. Such a franchise is usually the key to sustained high returns.'

There speaks the voice of experience, and an incredibly successful experience at that. We ignore it at our peril. Dozens of examples of deal-making companies spring to mind as I read Buffett's words, companies who are forever gobbling up new businesses and tacking them onto their existing empire with little regard as to how, or even whether, they mesh together. It is like some adult game of Pass the Parcel. As long as the music keeps going and the

---

After the Crash, when a job in the City became less of the secure thing it had once been, it became almost dangerous for employees to take a day off sick.

One chap of modest years had greatly impressed his employers, working hard on the phone even when his less dedicated colleagues seemed to have nothing to do, bidding aggressively for stock and showing a great deal of enthusiasm for his job.

But he was eventually ill and, unfortunately, a problem arose with one of his deals while he was away. His bosses knew they would be able to solve it quickly by replaying the tape recording of the employee's conversations. This is what they heard: 'I'll bid you a penny better . . . At the first stroke it will be 11:50 and 50 seconds . . . Come on, you know you won't do better anywhere else . . . At the first stroke it will be . . .'

It wasn't all like that. Some of it contained the cricket scores and the recipe of the day as well as the rather one-sided conversation. On his return to work, the chap found his P45 waiting for him.

parcel keeps getting shuffled along the line, changing shape all the time, everything is okay. There is no time to examine it closely. But when the music stops, the whole thing can blow up in everybody's face.

Several well-known companies, formerly darlings of the City, had been using their highly-rated shares to build their empires in the pre-Crash days. Come the collapse in share prices and the game was suddenly over, leaving them stuck with a company made up of a rag-bag of businesses that nobody in their right mind would have assembled if they had been starting out from scratch. Lovely though they may look at first sight, the Emperor's new clothes will probably come unravelled eventually.

Unfortunately, Buffett's view that excitement and change are not synonymous with investment success is very far from being universally held. Companies which stick doggedly to their last may find investors turning their backs and seeking something with a little more glamour. In days gone by, this might not have mattered too much, for the directors could probably have assumed that good results would speak for themselves and would eventually improve the perception of their shares. In these days of short-termism, on the part of companies as well as investors, such long-term thinking is a luxury that many boards believe they cannot afford.

For investors' sakes, one hopes that they don't take the most drastic solution and begin a spate of takeover bids left, right and centre to distract attention from what is really going on. There is another route also frequently taken by companies, one which we can follow by eavesdropping on the boardroom. The quality of the bugging device used is not good enough to be able to distinguish who is talking.

A: It's ludicrous. Our profits have risen each year for the

past eleven. So have our earnings and dividends. Yet our rating is far below the market average. What do they want? Blood?

B: Perhaps we should give it to them and all throw ourselves out of the window. The City might take a little notice of that.

A: Perhaps you should go boil your head.

B: I should like that remark to be struck from the minutes . . .

A: I'll strike you from the minutes in a moment.

C: Gentlemen, I think I may have the solution. (Sound of chins hitting the tabletop as mouths drop open.) It's our image that is the problem. We come across as being a fuddy-duddy family engineering firm. That's what's conjured up in the mind whenever the name of Wilberforce's Wonderful Widgets is mentioned in the City, or perhaps I should say, *if* Wilberforce's Wonderful Widgets is ever mentioned in the City.

A: Wilberforce's Wonderful Widgets was a good enough name for my father and grandfather and his father and grandfather before him. If you want to come up with anything different, it had better be bloody good, my lad.

C: I was thinking along the lines of something thrusting, go-ahead, something really 'nineties'. Let's show a bit of drive, determination and vitality. Er, how about WWW Group?

A: (pause). Throw him out of the window gentlemen, would you?

But, after thinking it over, WWW Group becomes the adopted name and Wilberforce's Wonderful Widgets is no more. Within a year, the company is on a higher than average market rating, the chairman has made the cover of Business Magazine and C's widow's shares are doing very nicely thank you. WWW still makes the same widgets as it did before and the board (with the exception of C, God rest his soul) is unchanged. The City, however, now realises just how dynamic the WWW Group really is.

You probably think I am jesting. I only wish I were. Why else would Metal Box change its name to MB Group or Rio Tinto Zinc to RTZ? Why else should Imperial Chemical Industries prefer to be known only as ICI? It would appear that in Britain's boardrooms initials are thought to be with-it and hip. Either that, or directors are simply hopeless at thinking up new names. You may be surprised at just how many quoted acronyms there are in the UK. If you can bear to read aloud the following companies, all listed on the Stock Exchange, see how many (if any) mean anything at all to you: A&M, AAF, AAH, AB, AC, AGB, AIM, AMEC, AMI, AMS, APV, ASD, ATA, BAA, BAT, BBA, BBB, BDA, BET, BHH, BICC, BM, BOC, BOM, BPB, BPP, BSG, BSR, BSS, BTP, BTR, BTS, CALA, CAP, CASE, CCA, CCF, CDFC, CH, CI, CLF, CML, CPC, CPU, DDT, DPCE, DRG, DSC, EBC, EIS, EMAP, ERF, F&H, FII, FKB, FKI, FR, GC, GEI, GKN, GPG, GR, HTV, IMI, INOCO, ISA, ITL, JS, JSB, KCA, KLP, LDH, LIT, LPA, LWT, M&G, MAI, MB, MEPC, MIL, MK, ML (Holdings), ML (Laboratories), MS, MTL, MTM, MY, NMC, NMW, PCT, PE, PML, RCO, RHP, RKF, RMC, RTZ, S&U, SAC, SEP, SI, SKF AB, SPP, STC, T&N, T&S, TACE, TDS, TGI, TI, TIP, TMD, TSB, TSL, TSW, UCL, UDO, UEI, UPL, UTC, VG, VPI, VSEL, WA, WB, WCRS, WPP, WRM, WSP.

No, I thought not. They are almost all completely anonymous. I halted only once on my way through, when I came to M&G which, let's face it, cheats a little by putting that interesting ampersand in the middle of its name and has, in any case, been going for quite a few years. The rest have no such excuse. What could be worse for a company than for it

House Scraps, the Victorian Stock Exchange scrapbook, lists the following nicknames for shares, in the days when initials were barely used at all.

Aylesbury Dairy Company	Ducks
The Chartered Bank of India, Australia and China	Pigtails
Manchester, Sheffield & Lincolnshire Railway Deferred Stock	Sarahs
Bryant & May	Matches
Barrett's Brewing & Bottling Company	Bottles
The London, Brighton & South-Western Railway	Berthas
Eastern Extension Telegraph	Chinas
The India Rubber, Gutta Percha & Telegraph Works Company	Silvers
Hotchkiss Ordnance Company	Kisses
The Sunchales Extension of the Buenos Aires & Rosario Railway Company	Sunshades
Varna & Rustchuk Railway 3 per cent. Obligations	Bulgarian Atrocities

to change a name that is actually in English and swop it for a set of two or three initials? Yet it is happening all the time. More and more are trying to give the impression that they are doing something exciting and challenging by changing their name, thus risking becoming complete nonentities. Instead of giving the impression of being exciting, they only convince me that they lack imagination and are nothing but a bunch of mindless sheep, doing what the others do because they can't think of anything better.

Goodness knows what happens to all the goodwill they have built up over the years under the old name while employees, salesmen, customers and investors try to grapple with the seemingly pointless change. I cannot imagine what goes on in some of the heads occupying Britain's boardrooms.

The Southampton, Isle of Wight and South of England Royal Mail Steam Packet Company may be something of a mouthful, but at least a name like that gives us a fair idea of what the firm is about. (Perhaps by the time this book has been published, it will be SIOWASOERMSPC.)

There is one American corporate acronym of which I am rather fond and where I am willing to concede that some thought went into its construction. It is NBI. It stands for Nothing But Initials!

The following poem touching upon the matter, appeared in the pages of the *Financial Times*.

> Oh BET! What XTC
> I always feel when UIC
> I used to rave o'er RTZ
> With LRC I went to bed.
> In BHP I put my cash,
> With BAT I cut a dash.
> For RMC and many more
> I was a keen competitor
> But now they're a non-NTT
> For UXL them all, UC.

A great deal of effort can be put into choosing names and a whole industry has arisen of 'consultants' who will advise companies. They are only too keen to point out how crucial it is to give a good first impression by having the right name for your company. Their services, of course, are not given gratis, so companies can end up spending a small fortune with nothing to show for it but a bunch of initials. Of course, if a company decides to change its name (or even to think one up in the first place) it does not have to opt for a set of initials. A whole string of companies at the sharp end of the technological revolution seem to think that they can show how brilliant they are by shoving 'micro' or 'tech' in somewhere. In America, they now use computers to generate names at random. International Harvester, for instance, sold its agricultural equipment business together with its well-known name and so had to come up with another. The computer produced 3,000, including such scintillating suggestions as Primerica, Intran, Alta and Amanex before ending up with Navistar International Corp. That was picked out by a group of shareholders, advertisers, employees and customers from the short-list. Ever heard of Varity Corporation? That's the old Massey Ferguson, risen from the ashes. Houston Natural Gas became Enteron and then Enron Corporation.

According to the chief executive of Lippincott & Margulies which thinks up names for companies (shouldn't

---

When British Telecom's shares were sold in Britain, they were launched simultaneously in several other stock markets around the world. One was Toronto, where the privatised utility's shares were given the symbol BTY.

Nobody had realised that there was already a stock in existence with that code, Beauty Counsellor International. Their shares shot from 25 cents to 65 cents before somebody realised the mistake and changed the symbols.

[124]

they have a look at theirs before charging other people good money?), the letter 'X' is one of the most powerful in the alphabet: 'It stands for excellence' apparently. He thought up Nynex, part of the old AT&T. US Steel, which most people must have heard of, changed its moniker to plain USX. I haven't seen any estimates of how much it costs a UK firm to change its name, but in America consultants' fees are said to range up to a quarter of a million pounds. Add on the expense of reprinting your stationery, repainting your vans and telling everybody what you have done and you are probably talking a tidy sum. Navistar have put their total expenditure as a result of the name change at over $13 million.

It may seem laughable, but let's not forget that this is all shareholders' money. When Burroughs and Sperry merged to form the second biggest computer group in the world, the firm decided it didn't need to splash out on hiring image consultants. Instead, it turned to its 100,000 employees, offering a prize of $5,000 for whoever chose the new name. There were 31,000 entries. Reading through some of the entries, such as AABSG International, Buros, Busper, Supurb, Squabb and Zyre, perhaps one should not be too snooty about Unisys, the name eventually picked. It was fortunate that they time-stamped entries for there were eleven that suggested the winning name.

The most common name-changer here was surely BL, or British Leyland, or BMC or the Rover Group or whatever. Did the frequent changes of title really improve its image in most Britons' minds? Or was it merely an attempt to conceal reality by papering over the cracks?

The Design Council hit out at companies in late 1987 for failing to pay enough attention to the design of their products. The chairman claimed that our trade imbalance would be far less serious if firms bothered to take a good look at the products on which their success or failure depended: 'Although there are some exemplary companies, the general standard of design management in companies in Britain is nothing like good enough . . . mediocrity in design is the rule.'

Yet although companies, if he is right, don't bother too much about what their products look like, they seem very concerned what the company itself looks like in the public's eye. A recent study looked into which 'major issues of growing importance' executives ranked mostly highly. Spurious and unimportant things like Cash Flow barely made it into the top ten. Even Financial Performance only made it onto the number two slot. No, most important of all in the opinion of the large British companies surveyed was Corporate Image.

I reckon that £7.5 million is a lot of money, even these days. I drool at the thought of what I could do with that sort of sum. So what did ICI spend their seven-and-a-half million smackers on? That's right, you win a coconut. They spent it on a campaign to discover and project a new image for the company which was seen in the UK as being 'dull, boring and chemical'. Abroad nobody seemed to have heard of it at all which must have been a little disappointing for Britain's biggest manufacturer.

The £7.5 million 'advertising and corporate image campaign', according to the burbling press release on this momentous occasion in September 1987, emphasised 'ICI's position as a major British company occupying a leading place in the high technology science-based industries of the world.'

This was the culmination of 'more than a year of intense market research and discussion aimed at producing up-to-date corporate advertising and a new house style.' Wolff Olins, a leading corporate identity consultancy group were

[126]

brought in. Their accepted recommendations involved the company shunning the pejorative word 'Imperial', opting for the usual trio of initials instead (how original!). And, as with so many other similar exercises, a new logo was produced.

In ICI's case, however, it looked almost exactly the same as the old one. To be fair, ICI's has been going for over sixty years. They don't demean it by calling it a logo though, or even a logogram. Initially it was known within the company's Trade Marks Department (I get all this from the press release) as 'The Circle and Wavy Lines Device'. It only took them until the 1950s to come up with the name 'Roundel'. You probably know what it looks like, the letters 'ICI' floating above some very imperial-looking (Sorry, wash my mouth out with soap) waves. The changes made to it on this earth-shaking occasion were staggering in their scope, as they ought to have been in the first redesign of the roundel for twenty years. Wolff Olins, after much putting together of heads and pencil-sucking, made the letters more solid and the waves less wavy. Nor was this all. In a dramatic move, probably unique in the annals of corporate identity history, the colours were swapped round. Instead of blue on white, the roundel is now white on blue.

According to ICI's very own Corporate Publicity and Marketing Adviser 'We believe the Company and its employees will gain from this exercise by the creation of a better "family feeling" – the modernised roundel symbolising the continuing value of the Company and being critically important in unifying the widespread and disparate businesses of ICI.'

Just so. And now, I imagine, there is nobody left anywhere in the world who still dares to think that ICI is 'dull, boring and chemical.' If you ask me, if they had really wanted to make an impact, they should have reverted to their old name of Explosives Trades Limited and the old trademark of a volcano doing its stuff. Do they, I wonder, make a product that helps wash hogs?

ICI, of course, is not the only company to undergo this sort of treatment. Only a few months earlier, investors and workers in Courtaulds had poured into the streets, banners held aloft, in a spontaneous demonstration of support for the company's new identity. Launched at the same time as Courtauld's Annual Report and Accounts, it involved a new symbol and a new typeface for company documents. The chairman, Sir Christopher Hogg, said (or else had it said for him by a PR person): 'Our new identity reflects the fundamental changes which have taken place in Courtaulds and gives expression to the new "culture" of our business. Innovation, quality in design and all-round professionalism are essential to our continuing success and we believe that it is also important to apply the same standards to all aspects of our communications.

'The new symbol, known as "the C-Mark", is designed to be distinctive, and to reflect the versatility of the group and the different characteristics of its businesses while at the same time recalling the initial letter "C".' The 'C-Mark' has some round bits, a triangle and some squiggly bits. The design and communications consultants worked on it for two years before it saw the light of day. According to the *Financial Times*: 'The asymmetry of the logo is an attempt by Lloyd Northover, the consultant, to convey the disparity of the Courtauld's group, yet give it some cohesion. The logo's combination of hard and soft lines is intended to suggest the group's marriage of technology with design and flair.' Viewing it much like those pieces of paper psychologists proffer to patients to see what images are conjured up in the mind's eye, it looks to my untutored gaze like the sail of a yacht glimpsed behind some cliffs somewhere near a London Transport station or bus stop. Perhaps in twenty years, they'll decide to reverse the colours, smooth out the waves, and give themselves another new identity.

It was very sensible of the Securities and Investments Board to set up a register so that investors can find out by phone or on Prestel whether particular investment advisers are authorised or not.

However, given the modern mania for turning everything into sets of initials, was it a wise choice to call it the Central Register of Authorised Persons?

Goodness knows how much BAA spent on its advertising budget when trying to educate the public about its change of name. The full page ads had a sheep at the top saying, 'BAA BAA', the idea apparently of the lateral thinker Dr Edward de Bono, who had bleated at the advertisers down a phone line from Toronto (all this is in the ad, I kid you not). 'I'm not going mad,' he informed them, 'It's quite simple. What I'm trying to do is get people to remember BAA as a noise rather than a set of initials.'

The problem for the company was that, under government control, it was the British Airports Authority. Privatised in 1987, it could no longer be an 'authority'.

'What else could our initials stand for? Alternatives like British Associated Airports and British Amalgamated Airports lacked the resonance the corporate soul so craves.

'Why not simply initials? After all, Harry S. Truman stood for President with a middle initial that didn't stand for anything. It certainly didn't stand in his way.' I would have been more interested in the erstwhile president if he had stood for office under the name of HST. People would have thought somebody was simply trying to attract their attention if Dr de Bono's methods had been applied.

Whether BAA achieved their aim in these expensive ads, I do not know. It is conceivable, of course, that as people sit kicking their heels in BAA airport lounges while the Spanish air traffic controllers take a four-day siesta, their minds will turn to thoughts of sheep. Whether the images of animals being herded into crowded pens will help or hinder BAA's cause I cannot tell. The thought of the population of an entire departure lounge at Heathrow or Gatwick bleating like little lambs, as they read Dr de Bono's thoughts, is not one I would find particularly appealing. The company's telephonists certainly don't do so. They are very careful to voice the initials distinctly.

APV (another set of initials) drew a lot of ribald attention to itself in 1988 with its full page ads featuring male and female nudes cavorting about on top of a sideboard, or at least that is what it looked like. In one, a baby, was being held aloft as well. What that had to do with food manufacturing equipment, chemical and polymer processing machinery, or the making of printing equipment is totally beyond me. Still, it did give APV a certain amount of notoriety for a little while. Not only was it able to get full-page nudes in the quality national papers, but the campaign also aroused excitement in the more sensational tabloids.

I know, I know. I am stuffy and boring, hidebound and old-fashioned. Yet I cannot understand the point of some of these image-building exercises, unless it is to provide work for consultants or to pamper the egos of the directors of the companies concerned. I hate to think of the money spent on new logos by those otherwise sane companies BT and BP in the face of ridicule from the general public. No doubt it makes the corporate consultants – and their bankers – extremely happy.

Names may well be very important to the public perception of a company, but there is some, extremely unscientific, evidence that the modern 'sexy' names being chosen by so many firms may be a positive turn-off to investors. Oofy Prosser, esteemed City columnist in *Punch* magazine, was tiring of those investors who began to pant and let their tongue hang out whenever they heard of companies with 'electronic' or 'computer' or 'exploration' or 'bio-technology' in their titles and so put together a list of 17 companies whose names were extremely unattractive. They were chosen for this reason alone, with the investment merits of each company irrelevant. The 'Portfolio of Dogs' consisted of the following household names: 'Baggeridge Brick, Biddle Holdings, Brickhouse Dudley, Castings, Downiebrae, Elswick Hopper, Foseco Minsep, Hicking Pentacost, Lincroft Kilgour, Newman-Tonks, Peglar-Hattersley, Phicom, Ruberoid, Shorrock, Thurgar Bardex, Volex and Whatman Reeve Angel'.

The portfolio was begun at the start of 1986, a year in which the stock market as a whole rose by 15%. The Portfolio of Dogs, on the other hand, sprinted ahead, finishing the year with an average rise of 61%! It had been helped by the odd bid or two, to be sure, but was still an extraordinary performance considering the random way in which they were chosen.

Sadly, the 'Dogs' were put to sleep humanely at the beginning of 1987, so we have no record of how they would have done had they been allowed to continue their existence, nor any idea of just why they should have done so well in their short lifetime. It is interesting to note that one or two of them have since undergone name changes, thus disqualifying themselves from any such future portfolio!

8

Paper, Paper Everywhere

Time was when the only communication private investors got as a result of their shareholding was a rather dull and drab Annual Report that looked as though it was put together with a John Bull Printing Set. Now we get not only brilliantly glossy financial documents from our companies, but all manner of junk mail from every other possible direction as well.

Image now obsesses companies in their shareholder communications as in everything else. You can hardly pick up an Annual Report now without coming across some asinine slogan purporting to express the company's philosophy in a nutshell: 'A Year of Dynamic Growth' (FKI); 'Progress Through Partnership' (Redland); 'Successfully Managing Change' (Burton); Marks & Spencer tried 'Investment in Progress' and 'Sharing in Success' before settling on 'Quality and Value Worldwide'. They are far too boring and squirm-inducing for me to want to inflict any more of them on you. There must surely be a limit to the number of these things you can think up using just three or four words. How they avoid using slogans used by other companies is beyond me.

Still, at least the old days of grey, anonymous covers and columns of interminable figures are long gone for the majority of companies. Instead, we have gloriously colourful photographs, charts and diagrams that often make the Annual Report look more like a magazine than a statutory financial document. In fact that was exactly the intention with the 1986 Burton Group Annual Report which, with its hundreds of photographs (literally!), more closely resembled *Vogue* or *Harpers & Queen* than the usual company report.

Burton is one of the companies spearheading the change in corporate communications. Like many pioneers in the vanguard of this change, it realises that its shareholders may also be customers of the group. This is why the retail groups have made such immense efforts over the past few years with their Annual Reports. In some cases, they have practically been sales brochures, so direct has their approach been. One of the Burton's interim reports had a Freephone number which shareholders could ring at any time of day or night in order to buy any of the Harvey Nichols' items worn by the models appearing in its pages, such as Roland Klein silk dresses or a shocking pink taffeta jacket by Rifat Ozbek. One of the poor girls was even clad in a bedspread (£169) and embroidered double sheet (£74), holding a cushion (£38) with an upturned pink lampshade (£57) perched rather precariously on her head!

Yet although Burton has come in for some ridicule for its way-out Annual Reports, the fact that it persists in trying to make them interesting presumably means it feels that they are achieving their impact. Its 1987 Annual Report was not only once more lavishly illustrated, but was also double the conventional A4 size adopted for such documents.

Companies find Annual Reports useful, not only in

[134]

communicating with shareholders, but also with employees, suppliers and customers. It is considered to be a very effective marketing tool. And it isn't only the retail groups who are blazing a trail with Annual Reports. Design and advertising firms also tend to use their Reports to promote their own wares. The Michael Peters design group, which produces many Annual Reports for other companies, has blazed some trails in its own documents. It produced the first-ever Pop-up Annual Report in 1984, a masterpiece of paper engineering. I foolishly gave my copy away to a young lady I was trying to impress (unsuccessfully), only to discover recently that copies in mint condition have changed hands for around £200!

Question: What is the difference between a gilt and a gilts dealer?
Answer: The gilt eventually matures.

Michael Peters also produced its original prospectus in the form of an origami kit (before the Stock Exchange brought in its pathetic new rules) and its interim results each year are printed on the back of beautiful limited edition colour prints. There is even some talk of using video tapes to get the message across in future years.

Prestwich Holdings is another firm using its Annual Report in an imaginative way. The company is involved in the mass entertainment and leisure markets and has sprinkled its 1987 Report with some of the characters that feature in its products, such as videos and T-shirts. Mickey Mouse is on the cover, along with Minnie, while Pluto also makes an appearance. This must be the only board of directors who have appeared in their accounts pictured in Fred Flintstone's car! (Fred was driving at the time). Although it sounds frivolous, it was a very imaginative way to project just what the company did.

Companies in less glamorous industries may still find ways in which to use their Annual Report as a sort of shop window. As printing materials group Wolstenholme Rink explained, the printing and packaging of its 1986 Report and Accounts 'involved the use of several Group products. These include: Hot Sampling Foil (used on the gold envelope and on the cover of the Report & Accounts), Bronze Powders (used in the gold ink to print the envelope and the text pages of the Report & Accounts), Thermographic Powder (used in the production of the red seal on the envelope) and Printing Products (used on the press which printed the Report and Accounts)'. It was all pretty garish, but none the less effective for that.

The most innovative Reports frequently meet with an adverse reaction in the City, where the Accounts snobs turn their nose up at them. The attitude often taken there is that the figures are the only things that matter and that all the gloss is superfluous and merely detracts from the numbers. It may even be used to conceal or draw attention away from unpalatable data. Design, they say, is no substitute for detail.

For the majority of investors, though, the new style Annual Report must surely come as something of a godsend, providing it doesn't go too far over the top. Most Reports are believed to go straight into the waste-paper bin, without so much as a cursory glance. Anything that stays an investor's hand for a moment before he casts an Annual Report into oblivion and which might persuade him to read it is to be encouraged. It may well be that an investor looks only at the photographs and reads nothing other than the

Chairman's Statement. Yet this, surely, is better than nothing?

However glossy the Report, the figures will still be there for the analysts and the fund managers to plough through and it seems churlish of them to object on aesthetic grounds alone. They are fortunate in being able to visit the companies in which they hold shares, to talk to the board and examine the products and plant directly. This is not an option usually open to private investors. Companies which help increase investor understanding about their activities through their Reports should be applauded, providing that what they are giving is extra information and not simply image and hot air.

It might be fairer to grumble about the cost involved in producing one of these glossy documents. For they don't come cheap. A small company may have to pay around £20,000 or £5 a copy for each of its Annual Reports, while a largish firm may end up spending a hundred thousand pounds or more.

Of course the figures are important. But there is more chance of an investor new to the stock market attempting to understand the figures if his attention has been arrested and aroused by the rest of the Accounts. If it is simply thrown out, to go soggy under a heap of potato peelings, then no-one but the odd fly will get a glimpse of the figures at all.

If we are ever to have a true shareowning democracy in this country, then it is vital that a greater number of private investors understand at least the basic figures contained within the Annual Report. Through knowledge lies strength, and all that jazz.

The Department of Trade and Industry, however, has other ideas. In its wisdom, it has decided to allow companies to send out slimmed-down versions of Annual

It isn't easy for the big privatised companies, having to cope with a share register of millions of investors. One TSB shareholder wrote to the *Financial Times* complaining that, although he and his wife held just 7,700 shares in the company, they had received seven copies of the bank's Annual Report and had been sent seven dividend cheques.

With the biggest share register in the country, it is understandable that British Gas refrained from sending out 'Welcome to British Gas' letters to its 3.3 million initial shareholders. For many of them, this was the first share they had ever held. Such a shame, then, that the first communication they received was a demand for the second payment on the shares.

Someone at British Gas, in an idle moment, worked out that those 3.3 million copies of the 1987 Annual Report would make a stack four-and-three-quarter miles high.

Reports. The pressure for this move has come from the largest of the privatised companies, with TSB the ringleader. Cost is obviously one factor in their wish to have shortened Reports. TSB has, at the time of writing, almost two million shareholders. In 1987 it spent £1.7 million on sending out its Annual Report although, presumably, it got some of this back as it also takes the opportunity of its shareholder mailings to enclose promotional material for various financial services, such as the TSB Homebuyer's Mortgage, TSB Personal Loans, TSB Home Contents Insurance, TSB Travel Insurance, TSB Trustcard, Swan National Car & Van Rental. After sending out its first Report, TSB received a quarter of a million enquiries. Presumably some business resulted to offset the cost of the statutory shareholder information?

Yet the bank also believes that the majority of its shareholders would prefer to receive abbreviated Accounts. A straw poll at one of TSB's regional shareholder meetings found two-thirds of those voting in favour of the move. This may indeed be the view of the majority of new investors who, perhaps, do not realise how important to the health of their investment those figures are, but it is doubtful if the same would be true of more experienced hands. Although the opinions of companies and institutional investors were canvassed by the DTI before making its announcement, it would appear that no private investors – the very group the Government has said over and over again it wants to encourage – were consulted. The move was simply presented as a *fait accompli*.

To say that most private investors would prefer to receive the shortened version is a little like saying that most children would prefer not to go to school. Allowing them to opt out would no doubt save a great deal of money. Yet that is not a good argument for denying them education. I have yet to hear any good arguments for denying shareholders the full financial information on their companies.

The Department of Trade, for its part, argues that any shareholder who wants the full version will be free to ask for it. Just imagine the time involved in arranging to receive the full reports if you have a substantial portfolio. This is the same system as used in the United States although, interestingly, the Australians insist on the unabridged version being sent out unless investors ask for the shortened one. Many of the large companies have already adopted abbreviated Accounts and, despite being lavishly illustrated with mugshots of the directors and the companies' activities, only the briefest of financial information is given. This may well be all many shareholders want when they are relative newcomers to the stock market, but should they ever be curious enough to want to delve into the back of an Annual Report, their curiosity is likely to have evaporated by the time the company responds to their requests for the unabridged version.

A company's auditors will examine the detailed figures in the main Accounts and confirm that they give a 'true and fair view' of the company's affairs. But they need not concern themselves with the abbreviated Accounts and it is surely possible to present a rosy picture of even the most troubled company. What is left out could be the stuff that it is most important for shareholders to read. Indeed TSB's abbreviated financial statement warns that 'it does not contain sufficient information to allow for a full understanding of the results of the Group and state of affairs of the Company or of the Group'.

I would have thought it far more sensible for the DTI to be trying to find ways in which to make full financial statements intelligible to the majority of human beings rather than cutting back on the information sent out simply because we are not all budding stockbrokers' analysts. If the Government want a shareowning democracy, why don't they insist that schools teach the understanding of Annual Reports as part of the curriculum? It would be a very valuable skill in future life, just as it would be useful to be taught how to read the small print of insurance and pension documents.

Presumably it will only be private investors who are sent the Janet and John version of the Accounts ('This is WWW Holdings, Children. Say hello to WWW's cheerful chairman, Sir Charles Chaffinch. He's done wonders with your money in the past year. Say thank you to Sir Charles, children'). I can't imagine the big institutional investors taking too kindly to receiving the abbreviated documents, nor can I believe that the Pru will want to have to ring up to get a full Report on every company in which it has shares.

One of the principal pillars of the UK stock market is that all shareholders should be treated equally. The DTI's move is, instead, splitting us up into two classes of shareholders

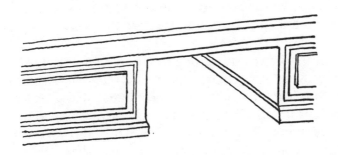

with, to paraphrase Orwell, some treated more equally than others. It is the big privatised companies like TSB, British Gas, BT and the water and electricity companies, with literally millions of uninformed investors on their books, that are likeliest to opt for abbreviated Reports. Yet while they may be perfectly trustworthy, there must be other, smaller, companies who look on the decision as giving them an excellent opportunity for muddying still further the picture given to shareholders.

Some 400 tonnes of paper were used in the sell-off of British Telecom. By the time of TSB, this figure had risen to 700 tonnes, while British Gas used 1,300 tonnes. The collapse in the stock market in October 1987 did not come quickly enough for the trees, hit not only by the hurricane, but also by the City's need for 2,000 tonnes of paper for the doomed BP flotation!

I find it rather sad that, as a result of the government's drive towards wider share ownership, many investors will, as a matter of course, receive less information about the companies they own. It is only really the privatised giants who can make a sensible argument in favour of the two classes of Annual Report. Why not compel any other companies wanting to go down that road to ask the permission of shareholders first?

If investors are only going to get an abbreviated Annual Report from their companies, it is all the more important that they learn to read the signs contained in the tea leaves. Bob Stovall, the Wall Street stock market expert whose interpretations of chairmen's statements appeared earlier, believes it is important to look at the pictures contained within Annual Reports. Bob wrote to me saying that: 'It's

[142]

not only the verbiage which is predictable in American Annual Reports, but also the artwork. When companies are doing well they have frequently published Annual Reports with the finest of photography, usually concentrated on irrelevant landscapes or works of art. Managements are photographed in club rooms or on grand staircases wearing their finest Saville Row clothing or the equivalent. After a hard year, such as currently being experienced by banks in California, Texas and other parts of the 'oil patch', the artwork is usually in black and white rather than in colour. More tellingly, the managements are photographed in their shirt sleeves rather than in their three-piece suits. Rather than sumptuous club rooms, the ambience is full of clutter, specifically plastic coffee cups and sandwich wrappers around the computer terminal.' This must surely apply just as much to British companies as to their American cousins.

Despite the greater effort being made with the appearance of Annual Reports these days, many companies do find it hard to talk to their shareholders. There is still relatively little recognition in the boardrooms of the land that shareholders are the owners of the companies for which the directors work and that, rather than talking down to their investors, they should be talking up to them.

As one leading financial public relations adviser once confided to me, there are only two main questions that all investors or potential investors want to know about a company: 'Why buy the shares?' and 'Why hang onto them?' Yet the vast majority of companies shuffle their feet and shy away from such embarrassingly direct topics. It may even be possible to argue that under the wonderful Financial Services Act ('let's put everybody in straitjackets and then no-one will get hurt') companies cannot even address such subjects without becoming properly authorised persons. Yet that, surely, is going a little far.

It is often puzzling what lies behind movements in the prices, not only of shares, but of various commodities.

At the time of a flare-up in tension in the Gulf, ITN sent cameras along to the International Petroleum Exchange to film the price of oil soaring. It was, of course, doing nothing of the sort. The traders were lolling around in the pits with nothing to do. They hadn't even got their jackets on, so lax was business.

The IPE officials didn't relish the prospect of such pictures appearing on national television and pleaded with the traders to put on a bit of a show. So, reluctantly, they donned their coats and simulated an odd trade or two.

Initially, it all looked rather contrived but, as the cameras began whirring, those watching suddenly realised that the trading was beginning to get more exciting and that the dealers were actually transacting business with each other.

Convinced that, if ITN's cameras were there, something really important must be happening in the Gulf, the dealers pushed the price of gasoil futures up a not insignificant 20 cents. That's the power of the media for you.

American companies are far less restrained in their communications with their shareholders. Most of the Annual Reports in the United States start with a statement about 'shareholder objectives', showing what the directors are hoping to do with the company and how it should benefit investors. Some issue videos about their company free to shareholders, even including leading analysts talking about the attractions of the shares! The Annual Report of the Sara Lee Corporation (Electrolux, Fuller Brush, Kiwi, Radox and Rennie) begins 'Dear Stockholder'. That phrase alone puts Sara Lee in a different class from the majority of UK companies. It then explains that 'Sara Lee Corporation's mission is to be a leading consumer marketing company in the United States and internationally.'

[144]

Although grandiose corporate statements like this are not uncommon over here, the next bit is much rarer on this side of the Atlantic. 'Our primary goal is to maximise the long-term financial performance of the corporation, thus creating stockholder value and enabling us to better serve our employees, customers and the communities in which we do business . . . The creation of stockholder value requires that management develop the appropriate operating and financial goals and strategies necessary to identify and realise profitable growth opportunities. Two key financial indicators which reflect this ability to direct profitable growth are return on equity and real earnings growth. Our goals for these indicators are as follows:

- Maintain a return on equity of at least 20%
- Achieve real earnings growth of at least 6% pa over time.

'Stockholder value is realised in the form of dividends and changes in stock price. The best measure of management's performance is the increase in stockholder value over time relative to alternative investment opportunities.' This is accompanied by a chart showing how Sara Lee's performance compares not only with the stock market as a whole but also with US Treasury Bills over a 1, 5 and 10 year period.

By telling shareholders exactly what it intends doing over the coming years, the board is laying itself open to criticism if it fails to achieve its set targets. Yet this ought to be the way things are done. How can investors judge how successful their boards are, if they have little idea of their plans for the future? Not all British companies are lily-livered. For example, the 1988 Report of FKI (Grr! Hate those initials) began with the following Corporate

Statement: 'We are a diversified international engineering group committed to achieving consistent annual growth in earnings per share in excess of 25% for our shareholders by a combination of organic growth and selective acquisitions. We specialise in acquiring poorly-performing companies with good products and enabling them to fulfil their true potential.

'This policy has produced record profits for the fifteenth successive year and average compound earnings per share growth of 88% per annum over the last five years.'

Whether those companies that stick their neck out in this way will be quite so forthright and forthcoming in the wake of the recession will be interesting. But although City cynics may scoff at such statements from companies, as far as I am concerned the more they tell us in plain English about their intentions, the happier I shall be.

I prefer things to be in black and white and, unfortunately, an increasing amount of the information given in the form of figures in Annual Reports is needlessly obscure, not to say downright misleading. Accountancy firm Arthur Young threw a fairly substantial stone into a pond of complacency when, early in 1988, it called for a body similar to the Takeover Panel to help improve the quality of accounting. The present system, it claims, often enables companies to distort their figures. Heaven forbid! If a leading accountancy firm goes as far as this, then it is clear that something is rotten in the state of Denmark, and it isn't as trivial as a dead rat behind the skirting board. The *Financial Times* claims that 'it is easy to drive a coach and horses through accounting rules. The present method of setting and enforcing standards simply cannot cope with the ranks of devious directors, creative financiers and sharp lawyers who, between them, have made fiction of some companies' published financial information.'

[146]

Two books have been published on the subject of creative accounting. The dust jacket of one pointed out that although 'the figures on a balance sheet or profit and loss account should be an accurate reflection of company performance, they may have been adjusted in the interests of "public image" or to gain tax benefits. New accounting techniques mean figures can be presented to maximum advantage.' The authority of the other, Ian Griffiths, writing in *The Shareholder*, claimed that 'Annual Reports are no longer a representation of the year but simply a vague approximation of events of the previous 12 months.' Although such books on creative accounting can help investors to find a path through the minefield of the Annual Report (and possibly help finance directors think up new dodges), it does not say much for the present system that they are necessary at all. As Griffiths concludes: 'Blessed is the shareholder who expects nothing from a set of accounts for he shall not be disappointed.'

What is worse is that when companies set out to avoid creative accounting, the City may actually penalise them for doing so. The most famous instance of this is when, in the summer of 1987, the Argyll Group announced its results. Earlier in the year it had brought the Safeway supermarket chain but, instead of using creative accounting to hide the costs of integrating its new acquisition, it decided to be more up-front about it. Instead of charging the costs of integration below the line, as a one-off 'extraordinary' item which would have had no effect on profits or earnings per share, it took it instead as an 'exceptional' item, deducting the £90 million costs from pre-tax profits over four years.

Whichever treatment the company had taken, the amount of money it had to spend on sorting out Safeway would have been exactly the same. The acquisition had

Stockbroking analysts have changed little over the past hundred years. It was just before the turn of the Century that one Wall-Street broker issued a circular confidently informing clients that 'Signor Marconi's ingenious ideas do not seem to have made much headway. The public will be well advised to keep clear of this concern.'

taken place months earlier, and the costs were pretty much in line with the City's expectations. But because the profits appeared to be lower the way Argyll treated the acquisition, almost 10 per cent was wiped off the shares in just one day. So much for the expertise of the City's analysts.

Takeovers provide one of the most fruitful veins to be mined by the creative accountants. There are two ways in which companies can treat acquisitions. One is to use *merger accounting*. In essence, the company is able to add on the entire year's profits of the acquired company, even if it only bought it late in its financial year. This does not happen with the alternative treatment, *acquisition accounting*, another difference being that under the latter companies have to revalue the acquired assets at market value. If the value is much above their book value then the extra depreciation will hit profits and earnings. Any goodwill (the amount by which the purchase price exceeds the real value of the assets) must be written off under *acquisition accounting*. This too will hit earnings.

There are no prizes for guessing which method is used by most go-go companies, including some of the biggest firms in the land. Yet according to the accountancy bodies, both are perfectly acceptable, even though two companies making identical acquisitions can have radically different profits and earnings profiles if one *merger accounts* and the other *acquisition accounts.*

Another popular trick is to keep important items out of the Accounts altogether. Off-balance sheet financing can allow companies to keep investors completely in ignorance of important debts. When, in 1987, S&W Berisford decided to abandon its off-balance sheet accounting, debts of £52 million for which the company was ultimately responsible suddenly appeared from out of thin air.

The tricks companies can play with their figures are many and varied. The Institute of Chartered Accountants in England and Wales publishes an annual survey of Reports and Accounts. In its 1987–88 issue, it criticised some of the biggest companies in Britain. Hanson got a ticking off for not giving enough information about the performance of its constituent business, Trafalgar House was admonished for channelling costs through reserves instead of setting them off against profits, Vickers and Reckitt & Colman had the finger wagged at them for taking reorganisation costs below the line (unlike Argyll) so leaving their profits and earnings unblemished. The report was generally unhappy about the way in which most firms treated takeovers.

Some big name companies, which on the face of it had been doing well, came croppers in the recession of 1990–91. The majority of those whose sudden troubles surprised the market had been indulging in excessive creative accounting.

It would appear that creative accounting can paper over the cracks only while things are generally going well. As soon as recession hits, gaping holes in a company's fabric are suddenly revealed. Those fuddy-duddies who refused to be taken in by creative accounting and who insisted that they know the company's position with regard to real solid cash were proven right.

It beats me, though, how the individual investor (unless a fully qualified accountant) can hope to understand the real picture, even if he ploughs through every single note to the accounts. He can only hope that some sly footwork by a company in which he is interested will be spotted and publicised in the City pages. This hardly seems an ideal situation. If financial advisers are so wizard at thinking up new schemes to bend accounting rules, why can't equally devious minds be turned to the problem of simplifying financial reporting. For only if it is simplified will it become truly difficult for companies to deceive the readers of the Annual Reports.

As for those firms sending out abbreviated Accounts, the mind fairly boggles at the conjuring tricks they will be able to get away with. I sometimes wonder whether the reason the accountancy bodies are dragging their heels is because the members of their profession derive so much work as a result of creative accounting. (Go and stand in the corner, boy. What an evil mind.) Perhaps the Stock Exchange should use its considerable weight to sit on some of the more outrageous practices.

Some of the more sceptical users of Annual Reports claim that there are several tell-tale signs which can give the

---

An American financial planning consultant came up with what he reckons is a cast-iron way of telling when an investment has hit its peak. He studies advertisements. Harold Gourgues is the originator of the Gourdes Ad-Index, compiled by counting the number of full page ads for various types of investment in a leading magazine for intermediaries.

When one investment type claims more than 30% of the total, it is time to sell.

observer early warning of a company's possible insolvency. Here are some of the best-known insolvency clues, although I should stress that they are not infallible.

1. A photograph in the Annual Report of the chairman alighting from or entering a helicopter which the company has just bought.

2. A fountain in the reception area.

3. The directors' luxury cars have personalised number plates. (If they show a photograph of these in their Annual Report, they deserve what is coming to them.)

4. Political visits. The higher the rank of the visiting politician, the greater the risk. A photo of the Prime Minister opening, visiting, blessing or giving anything connected with the firm is the kiss of death.

5. A flagpole outside the headquarters.

6. The receipt of the Queen's award for industry (UK only).

7. The chairman honoured for services to industry.

8. The company wins an award for the best report and accounts.

9. The company announces that it is opening an office in China.

10. The company has a satisfied workforce with no strike record.

Not all mail coming through an investor's letterbox as a result of a shareholding is from those companies in which he has invested. As all of us now know, we are considered sitting ducks for the junk mailers. Groaning under the weight of sackfuls of unsolicited glossy brochures and enticing blandishments for all manner of things, the nation's postmen must curse the shareholding revolution. Many shareholders have cursed the companies or registrars who allow share registers to be used in this way. Some even claim to have sold their shares in protest.

Yet the companies cannot be blamed. For once, the finger points unerringly to Parliament and the clauses of the Companies Act. This sets out that a company's share register shall be open to inspection to any shareholder without charge and to anyone else for the payment of the appropriate fee. The fee is '5 pence or such less sum as the company may prescribe for each inspection.'

After the 1984 Olympics, the American medal winners got a tickertape welcome in New York. Amongst the paper to fall to ground in the Wall Street financial district were computer printouts listing the clients of broker Bear, Stearns & Co, together with their names and addresses, transactions, and portfolio details.

Brokers who had been idly watching the parade went berserk and started chasing this stuff all over the place, bundling the captured sheets up in their arms, realising just how much the material could be worth to them.

The managing partner of Bear Stearns, Alvin Einbender, said that 'It was an act of mischievous vandalism. I haven't caught the person who did it, but if I did and we were an Islamic country, we would probably punish him suitably.'

The direct mail people are hardly going to find it convenient sitting in front of the register writing down all the names and addresses it contains. But the Act also provides that anyone can ask for 'a copy of the share register, or any part of it, on payment of the appropriate charge . . . 10

pence or such less sum as the company may prescribe, for every 100 words (or fraction of 100 words) required to be copied.' Refusal to comply within ten days leaves the company and every officer of it liable to a fine. The rule was obviously introduced so that those investors needing to communicate with other shareholders in the company could do so. The charges were fixed back in 1948 and have not been amended since.

People's Capitalism has made the Companies Act in urgent need of amendment. But even if it is changed, the lists of shareholders' names and addresses are now widely circulated, and are being bought up all the time by insurance groups, timeshare operators, credit card companies, banks, building societies, car companies, indeed by anybody who considers that shareholders might be potential consumers of their product. One leading database operator selling shareholder lists charges upwards of £60 for a thousand names and addresses. Purchasers can pick investors depending on which companies they hold shares in, how many stock market investments they have, by their sex, age, affluence or where they live. The names and addresses will be provided for them on sticky labels ready to set in motion yet another junk mail operation. TSB should be praised for its outright refusal to hand its list to the direct mailers.

The bigger privatised companies have been pressing the Conservative Government to change the rules. Why it is dragging its heels on this is a mystery. It certainly can't be because it does not understand how the system works. On the contrary, guess which political party has sent unsolicited mail to almost half a million British Gas shareholders, seeking contributions to party funds?

Do people actually object to junk mail? A survey of consumers found that the majority are becoming increasingly irritated by it, with 70,000 asking to be taken off the junk mailers' lists in just one year, compared with 65,000 in the previous four years. On the other hand, a survey published just a few weeks later found that most people like direct mail and that more than two-thirds of people open and read everything that lands on their mat. That study, however, was published by the Royal Mail!

Those who do want to stem the flood of envelopes should write to The Mailing Preference Service at Freepost 22, London W1E 7EZ. You can tell them you want no more and all the organisations that support it will come to heel. You can also, if you wish, ask for *more* junk mail, or ask to receive glossy brochures only about particular products.

You may, like me, think that nobody in their right mind would do such a thing. Don't be sure. In one year, 9,288 people contacted the Mailing Preference Service to ask to receive extra junk mail.

9

Meet and Drink

Rude though I may be at times about directors, without someone to look after the shop for us there would be no company at all. It seems only sensible, therefore, that shareholders interested in the well-being of their investment would wish to go along to the company's Annual General Meeting. Only by doing so can they get a proper look at and a measure of the management in whose hands they have entrusted their company. Only by attending the meetings can they participate in the democratic process of shareowning. Only by getting to their feet in front of the directors can they make their voice heard.

Yet in reality the vast majority of Annual General Meetings are very sparsely attended. There is one overwhelmingly obvious reason for this. AGMs are almost all unbelievably tedious.

The general form is that you turn up at the venue, perhaps a rather dingy hotel conference room, to find a handful of old-age pensioners milling around picking up whatever brochures are given away. With a bit of luck, there will be a cup of coffee for you. With a bit more luck, there won't be, for it is usually ghastly muck. If you're early, your determination not to take it will soon wither for there is nothing else to do.

After reading the Annual Report for the umpteenth time, you are finally able to file into the hall where you plonk yourself down in a chair presumably designed as an instrument of torture (one of the few things at which British designers lead the world). Somewhere in the distant gloom is the board, arranged like ducks in a shooting gallery. Unfortunately, there is generally a pillar in the way so it is a little difficult to see what is happening. This doesn't seem to matter to the chap next to you. Although he has a clear view, his hearing aid isn't working so he gives up fairly early on and snoozes quite loudly, so that you now not only have problems seeing, but also hearing what is being said.

Fortunately, the proceedings don't take too long. The chairman stands up, thanks you for coming (though secretly wondering why you've bothered) and says a few exaggeratedly polite comments about the deadbeats on either side of him. He gives a glowing report about the company's progress which has shareholders hurriedly checking their Annual Reports for fear that they have come to the wrong meeting. He then asks for questions from the assembled shareholders before moving into the formal business of the meeting.

If there are any questions, they will usually be of the most trivial nature imaginable. Without wishing to be 'age-ist', it has always seemed to me that the more mature the shareholder, the more infantile and less relevant the question will be, always assuming that they can even phrase them in a way that is comprehensible to the rest of the meeting. The Chairman fields shareholders' questions about as expertly as a member of the England cricket team fields cricket balls, making you wonder what job the chap would ever be able to find if he should lose this one. Occasionally there is a question that really does hit home and which the board cannot sensibly answer. The Chairman will probably claim that the AGM is not the proper time to raise such a matter, and fob the shareholder off by suggesting that he write to him. The majority of the shareholders, who have only come in the first place because the only other source of free entertainment is the museums (who don't give coffee and biscuits) appear terribly embarrassed and hide their faces in the Report and Accounts.

The formal proceedings of the meeting then begin. Ten minutes later they are over and you find yourself filing out of the hall. If you are very fortunate, a glass of cheap sherry will be waiting for you outside. Even if you are foolish enough to accept a glass, it isn't long before you find yourself out in the open air again, wondering why on earth you wasted your time attending the meeting when you could have been doing something useful instead.

If you think that, in relating the above scene, I am exaggerating, then I can only imagine that you have never attended an Annual General Meeting. Generally speaking, the closer the company's activities impinge on its shareholders' lives, the greater the number of people who turn up for the meeting and the more interminable and idiotic the questions. There are times when I actually pity the chairmen of the privatised utilities like Gas and Telecom, having to field question after question about engineers who didn't arrive when they said they would or the company's failure to provide services to somebody living in a cave halfway up a sheer cliff.

Chairmen of retailing companies also seem to come in for a lot of stick, probably because every single person in the country believes themselves to be an expert on the subject. I

Not all Annual General Meetings are boring. The National Freight Consortium held its last meeting before seeking a flotation on the stock market at the Opera House in Blackpool. It was a somewhat jolly occasion, perhaps not altogether surprising considering that at that stage those employees who bought shares in the business back in 1982 had seen their investment mushroom to 60 times the original stake.

900 pensioners and about 3,000 employee/shareholders attended and were given a chance to make a weekend of it. In addition to the formal business of the meeting on the Sunday (where a crêche was provided, as well as a children's film show), those who were around on the Saturday could attend 'Bimbo's Magic Afternoon' or the pensioner's tea dance. The evening was rounded off with a Victorian Music Hall Evening starring Roy Hudd with various members of the board, including the chairman, strolling onto the stage in top hats and tails to sing 'Keep Right On To The End Of The Road.'

I can think of no other AGM where the chairman has had to interrupt the formal proceedings in order to inform two sets of parents that their offspring were crying inconsolably in the crêche and to ask them to try to remedy the situation!

still recall with a shudder one Annual Meeting of the Burton Group. One lady spent at least ten minutes complaining, somewhat incoherently, about a pair of curtains from Debenhams which did not fit properly. She would not be headed off, even though the rest of the meeting began to find her comments funnier and funnier. Sir Ralph Halpern was courtesy itself, although one suspected his tongue was some way into his cheek when he passed the buck on, suggesting that she stay to lunch and 'discuss it with the director concerned in detail.' So obsequious was he that I would not have been surprised if he had volunteered to come along and measure the things himself.

[158]

Other questions involved the lack of female directors of the board, the size of the Annual Report, the unfair dismissal of someone's son, the size of the Debenhams' pensioners' Christmas box, a store's fire safety record and the similarity of Sir Ralph and Sir Winston Churchill.

There was little that appeared to be directly concerned with the financial affairs of the company and, in that, the meeting was fairly typical of the majority of AGMs.

To some extent, the dullness of, and lack of attendance at, meetings can be blamed upon the companies. It is difficult for many people to take an hour or two out of the middle of the day if they are working so it is not surprising that most shareholders attending AGMs are retired. The attractions of free food and drink often seem more of a lure than the business of the meeting, too. You only need to go to one or two company meetings to realise that some people are professional AGM attenders, going year after year to practically every big meeting and judging their merits solely on the quality of the repast laid on afterwards. Those with jobs to go to are less likely to be willing, or able, to take time off just to get some free grub.

This isn't necessarily always the case. The London-based brewers, Young & Co, regularly have over a thousand shareholders attending their meetings, pretty impressive when you consider that that is around a quarter of the shareholder register. No doubt the free beer laid on is an incentive for some of the shareholders, yet the extraordinarily friendly atmosphere and the impression that you really are part of one big family, so different from most company meetings, must also be a big draw. Many of the shareholders have got to know each other over the years and the meeting has something of the feeling of a reunion about it. The last thing you feel at a Young's AGM is that the company does not care about you. On the contrary, the

Not all AGMs are as dull as ditchwater. The South London brewers, Young & Co, are able to entice a substantial proportion of their shareholders along each year, helped by the opportunity presented to sample the company's products gratis!

The meetings have progressed from a pub to the number eight cellar at the brewery, then to Wandsworth Town Hall and the West Centre hotel in Fulham before finally ending up in the massive ballroom of the Grosvenor House Hotel.

The first question of the chairman, John Young, at the 1987 AGM ran thus: 'I see from the accounts that you have taken a swingeing cut in your salary.

'Clearly, there are three possible explanations of this: the most prosaic being that it is a misprint; another that it is a self-imposed fine following repeated acts of gross immorality with members of your staff; the most likely, of course, is that you have taken a cut to keep the price of our pints down. I propose, therefore, to raise a hearty vote of thanks for that sacrifice.'

At the 1988 AGM, a shareholder caused consternation among the board when he claimed that the numbers in the Annual Report did not add up. In front of 1,300 shareholders, he pointed out, to considerable embarrassment on the part of the board and the auditors, that there was a discrepancy of £119,618 in the Source and Application of Funds ('Where the cash comes from and where it goes').

Yet despite the upset, due apparently to a printing error, the Annual Report was approved and the auditors reappointed.

Chairman goes out of his way to welcome people who have only one or two shares, believing that they are just as likely to be avid consumers of the brewery's products!

It is surprising how little effort most companies make to ensure that their AGMs are well-attended, leaving me with the distinct impression that many directors see the meetings as nothing more than an onerous chore, to be got through as quickly as possible so that they can return to the more serious business of running the company.

The times of AGMs might well be convenient to the board, but are they convenient to the shareholders? It would be interesting to see whether an evening meeting, or one held at the weekend would produce a greater attendance. Some troubled companies have gone entirely in the other direction, in the earnest hope that they will have as few shareholders attending as possible. The Christmas and New Year holiday period is a favourite time for the AGMs of companies in serious financial difficulties, afraid of detailed probing from those unfortunate enough to hold shares in the company. Alternatively, they might choose the Outer Hebrides as the most suitable spot to hold the meeting! Although it would be difficult for a large company to go out of its way to deter shareholders, by holding meetings at nine or ten o'clock in the morning some nevertheless rule out the attendance of any investor who has some way to travel, unless willing to fork out good cash for overnight accommodation.

If companies really were keen to get shareholders along then they ought to do more in the Annual Report to explain why they would like them to attend. Most Reports, of course, contain the notice of the meeting and a proxy card but nothing else in connection with the AGM at all. Yet considering the enormous sum now being spent on these documents, would it not make sense for the chairman to pen a letter explaining what is going to happen at the meeting and why he would welcome a good attendance? I realise that whatever efforts a company makes, the vast majority of AGMs will still be relatively dull occasions and I would not want to suggest that the chairman issue his board with red noses to enliven the proceedings. Yet most meetings are so unutterably banal that any change would surely be an improvement.

There can be no company in the land that can't run to a display showing shareholders the products and plant of the company in which they have invested. What excuse can there be for each board member not to turn up a little early to the meeting so that he or she can mingle with shareholders, having made sure that they are wearing identifying badges? They should be present after the meeting, too, for many individuals are bashful and, although having sensible questions to ask, may prefer not to stand up in front of strangers and to mouth them into a microphone.

Above all, the board should try to make the business of the meeting as interesting as possible. It is not surprising that few shareholders turn up if year in, year out, the proceedings are rushed through at the gallop and shareholders' questions are dismissed as being trivial or unimportant. Even if they are, the board should treat their betters with more respect.

Unless they make more effort with shareholder meetings, directors should not be too taken aback if attendance only soars when the company is in trouble, when the questioning from the floor is likely to be extremely hostile. A board that has taken more time and care over the years to cultivate its private shareholders may find them more readily willing to give the board the benefit of the doubt and less likely to be braying for the directors' blood.

Three meetings I attended come to mind as having elements that other companies should consider. One was Hillsdown Holdings, where the company had arranged for a range of its food products to be displayed in the foyer for shareholders to examine beforehand and where the chairman turned up to the meeting early, spending twenty minutes or so moving amongst shareholders, introducing himself and talking to as many as he could.

Another was the Merrydown Wine Company. No questions were asked at the AGM at all the year I attended, which surprised me. Seasoned attenders knew that there was really no necessity for, at the lunch that followed, there was at least one representative of the company at every single table.

There were questions in abundance at the meeting of Hanson I went to, which filled more seats in the concert hall at London's Barbican Centre than all but the most popular of orchestras. The standard of questioning, however, was far more intelligent than that at most company meetings and the ability of chairman Lord Hanson either to answer them succinctly himself or to pick on the director responsible meant that the meeting moved with breathtaking speed. The directors very publicly voted on all the resolutions before the meeting, holding their yellow shareholders' cards aloft as each vote was taken.

Yet despite a multitude of questions, the whole proceedings were over in just sixty-five minutes. Outside, the foyer was packed with stands at which Hanson's various subsidiaries were represented, many manned by fairly senior personnel. Showing shareholders the delights of Smith Corona's latest liquid crystal display typewriters was the chairman and chief executive of the recently-acquired American company himself.

Following the formal proceedings, Lord Hanson and Sir Gordon White positioned themselves on tall stools in the foyer and answered still more questions from shareholders, this time face to face.

One other thing which set this AGM apart from many others was the presence of a considerable number of UK and American fund managers. It is rare these days for the institutions to attend Annual Meetings. A senior fund manager boasted to me once that he had not attended an AGM for more than 15 years. He did not, however, con-

[163]

sider that he was lacking in his duty as a shareholder for, in common with other institutional investors, he was given plenty of other chances to meet the company's management and to quiz them on whatever aspect of the business he so wished.

The Stock Exchange has turned some of the floor space in their old regional Exchanges into Share Shops where you can seek information about investment in general, find out the latest share prices and so on, although not actually deal in them.

So popular was this with one chap that he went in every day and soon began to bring his Thermos and sandwiches with him. The patience of the staff with him finally snapped when he began receiving phone calls there. He had apparently left the number with several estate agents in case any suitable houses should come up!

If we have now reached the stage where fund managers almost never attend AGMs, because they feel that nothing of importance can possibly take place there (if they aren't present, the company would surely not dare make an interesting announcement), one can hardly blame private investors if they shun them too. Yet if shareholder democracy is to take root, something needs to be done to halt the decline in importance of the Annual General Meeting.

The main purpose of these meetings, of course, is to record the votes of the members of the company. Even the most popular of AGMs will still only be attended by a small minority of eligible shareholders. Although the rest can still make their views on the resolutions known by filling in their proxy cards, most of these end up in the waste paper bin, even if the Annual Report manages to avoid a similar fate.

[164]

When there is a very serious matter to come before an annual, or an extraordinary meeting, then the Board always seems to manage to find the time and the money to write to shareholders informing them why they want them to vote and recommending in which box they should put their cross. To my mind, it should be a matter of common courtesy for the board to explain to shareholders the importance of even the most routine of resolutions to be put before the meetings and to point out that, even if unable to attend personally, shareholders should still express their preferences on the enclosed cards. Yet, of course, in the vast majority of cases, no such effort is made, even though some resolutions which make regular appearances on proxy cards are written in hopelessly obscure language.

The adoption of the Report and Accounts, the declaration of the dividend and the re-election of directors are simple enough. But what about this Ordinary Resolution:

'That the directors be and they are hereby generally and unconditionally authorised for the purposes of Section 80 of the Companies Act 1985 ('The Act') to exercise all the powers of the Company to allot relevant securities (within the meaning of the said Section 80) of the Company during the period commencing on the date of the passing of this Resolution and expiring on the date of the next Annual General Meeting but so that the Company may before such expiry make offers or agreements which would or might require relevant securities to be allotted after such expiry and the directors may allot relevant securities in pursuance of such offers or agreements as if the authority conferred hereby had not expired provided that the nominal value of the relevant securities allotted pursuant to this authority shall not exceed the nominal value of the authorised but unissued share capital of the Company at the date of the passing of this Resolution.'

I make that 158 words in just one sentence, but I don't intend counting them again just to make sure. This is a fairly standard resolution and is always cropping up, although it is frequently expressed in fewer words, an indication perhaps that there is not only lawyerese for the shareholder to contend with, but bad lawyerese as well. In one instance at a meeting I attended this resolution took up 200 words. When it came to the vote, the Chairman's words were: 'This is a resolution to renew the company's power of allotment which is self-explanatory. I think that is the best way of putting it; it seems fairly complicated to me.' Referring to one of his own resolutions in an article in *The Shareholder*, the company secretary of British Gas wrote of one that was 250 words long by the time the lawyers had finished with it.

Some companies, particularly the privatised ones, do make an effort to explain the various resolutions when they send them to shareholders, although the explanations can be almost as confusing as the resolutions themselves. Sadly, such enlightened firms are few and far between.

The most common of these complicated resolutions to come up at AGMs will mention Section 80 or Section 95 (possibly 94 instead) of the Companies Act. The Section 80 resolution, put a little more simply than the lawyers are likely to, gives the board authority to issue extra shares up to a maximum stated amount and is usually valid till the following AGM.

Sections 94 and 95 are also concerned with the allotment of shares and will say something about Section 89, subsection 1, of the Companies Act not applying. Usually when issuing extra shares for cash, the company must stick to the pre-emption rules and give existing shareholders the first crack of the whip on a pro rata basis. This resolution allows the company to issue a certain number of shares as if this rule did not exist. Directors argue that it gives them a greater degree of flexibility than they would have if they had to go back to shareholders to ask permission each time they made a small acquisition.

Sometimes these rights are enshrined in the Articles of Association of a company, in which case any substantial changes in the sums would have to be accomplished by a change in the wording of those Articles.

Another popular number from the Companies Act to crop up from time to time is 163. A resolution including this Section will permit the company to purchase a limited number of its own shares in the stock market. Presumably this would be one instance where the board have a very good idea about the true financial state of the company in which they are investing. There is less chance of them having the wool pulled over their eyes. However, if their record of spending your money on acquisitions is truly terrible, this could be the time to get out.

Don't let the legalese used in wording resolutions for company meetings put you off voting. This is the one time when you really do have a say in the way your company is run. It is true, of course, that the big institutions' votes will far outweigh yours. With private investors owning under a fifth of all shares, our influence is relatively small. Yet we will never encourage companies to spend more time and effort on involving us in the business if we cannot show that we are interested. Even when the resolutions seem terribly dull and conventional, you should still make the effort to put your cross in the boxes and return the pre-paid card.

At least one company secretary I know asks the registrars

to forward any returned proxy cards that have comments from shareholders written on them. I do not know how widespread this practice is but, unlike ballot papers in elections, your vote is not invalidated if you write on the proxy card. So if you do have comments to make and are not able to willing or attend the meeting, why not scrawl them there and then, making sure of course that your voting intentions are still perfectly clear?

As part of its centenary celebrations in 1988, the *Financial Times* gave away a reproduction of the first ever issue. What a fascinating document it proved to be. In those days, the paper claimed on its masthead to be 'The friend of the honest financier, the bona fide investor, the respectable broker, the genuine director and the legitimate speculator' whilst declaring itself to be 'the enemy of the closed Stock Exchange, the unprincipled promoter, the company wrecker, the "guinea pig", the "bull", the "bear" and the gambling operator.'

One of the more fascinating titbits contained within it involves the 152nd half-yearly meeting of the Gas, Light and Coke Company, presided over by Colonel Makins, a Member of Parliament. Able to announce that the dividend was being raised to £41,000, Colonel Makins confidently told the meeting that 'he did not think that they had anything to fear from the electric light.'

If you do find time to go to an Annual General Meeting, or indeed any other company meeting, with the specific intention of asking a question, then do not be put off by the formality of the occasion. If you suspect you may be nervous of standing up in front of strangers, then write your question down first. It makes sense to keep it short and succinct. On the whole, those shareholders who ramble through four or five page treatises containing a dozen or more questions (and I have come across several of these odious creatures) will find they get very short shrift indeed from the board and that there is no sympathy at all for them amongst the other shareholders. If you suspect that your question is a very technical one which the board may not be able to answer off the tops of their heads, then perhaps it might be sensible to give the chairman prior warning. Questions about curtains that don't fit, or engineers that don't turn up are really only worth raising at AGMs if you have had no satisfaction from the ordinary complaints procedure open to any customer. An inability to deal with customer complaints is obviously important to the future profitability of any business. The fact that your wardrobe turned up ten minutes early while you were still having breakfast isn't likely to be.

If you believe the board to be a bunch of shifty, lying, cheating, good-for-nothings, an allegation that, for obvious reasons, you could hardly bring before the meeting, you could always try out an idea I have toyed with, but never had the guts to carry into practice. Seat yourself just a few rows back and, throughout the whole meeting, survey the assembled directors through a pair of binoculars or opera glasses. They can hardly fail to notice you and, if they have anything to feel guilty about, it cannot be long before they begin to feel distinctly uncomfortable and start squirming in their seats, trying all the while to avoid your searching gaze. I cannot guarantee the efficacy of this, but would be interested to hear from anybody who has the courage to try it out.

It is amazing just how forward some shareholders can be. In one famous incident, a chap leapt up onto the platform brandishing a tin of polish and a duster. He handed these over to the chairman of a leading High Street bank, demanding of the poor, bewildered, chap that he ensure

THE SHAREHOLDER

that the brass plate at his local branch be properly polished in future!

Most companies will now have public relations people wandering round before meetings trying to justify the massive fee they are being paid. So if you really are too nervous to ask your question in the meeting, it might be sensible to collar one of these people and ask if a director will listen to what you have to say either before or after the formal proceedings.

Not all companies are unhappy to see their shareholders by any means. It is usually the larger groups which put on a bit of a show for those who turn up; the famous packed Lonhro AGM is less an exercise in shareholder democracy than a Cecil B DeMille epic production. Yet some of the more enlightened minnows can still try to turn the event into something of an occasion. The food hamper company Park Food Group held an AGM in the directors' box of Tranmere Rovers Football Club. The managing director of the company happened to be chairman of the club and he had arranged for such idols of Tranmere's glorious history as Pongo Waring and Dixie Dean to be present. Sandell Perkins tempted its shareholders along to an AGM by holding it at Lord's cricket ground. Strong & Fisher, makers of leather clothing, held a fashion show at their AGM. And although hotels are the most favoured venue, oddities like the pump room in Cheltenham and the Botanical Gardens in Edgbaston have also been homes to company meetings.

Annual General Meetings are, by their very nature, held just once a year. But there is nothing to stop you writing to the company at any time to complain, compliment or criticise. The Chairman is probably the chap you should aim your missive at. The majority are rattling around in their big, plush, wood-panelled offices with little to do but practice putting golf balls into a glass, so they will no doubt welcome the opportunity of having a letter to reply to.

There are a few companies which get together with share-holders away from the AGM. The larger privatised companies, for instance, hold regional shareholder meetings at various locations around the country. These are rather more informal than the AGMs, and provide an opportunity for shareholders to meet and listen to directors and local managers.

The conglomerate, BET, is probably the most advanced in its promotion of shareholder open days, called 'The BET Experience.' These extravaganzas have been held in Leeds, Crawley and London's Docklands and are seen by the company as an opportunity to get together with its private shareholders who own a quarter of the company (a legacy of the days when it provided local tram and bus services), in an atmosphere something akin to a fun fair, demonstrating to them the wide range of the company's products. Although The Experiences cost around £100,000, share-holders are told that that is still less than a 30-second TV commercial or two press ads telling people how many of BET's cabinet towels it would take to reach the moon. Some of the cost is recouped when shareholders decide to buy double glazing or fitted bedrooms from the company.

Those who leave their wallets at home can try their luck at shattering double-glazed windows ('Have a go at breaking an Anglian Window! It's impossible') or entering the quiz. Winning it requires the shareholder to go round most of the exhibits, but the prizes, of two weeks on a BET safari in Kenya or a visit to the company's space flight simulator in Toronto, have usually been sufficient incentive. The Experience can attract over a thousand share-holders at a time, many of them also employees of the company for whom this is a chance to get a better idea of what the group as a whole is like.

BET's head of corporate communications, writing in *The Shareholder* Magazine, made it so obvious why the com-

[172]

Welsh stockbrokers Lyddon & Co, part of the National Investment Group, compiled an index composed of 30 quoted companies based in Wales.
  Its name? The Dai Jones index!

---

pany found these events worthwhile that it is all the more
baffling that more companies don't follow suit: 'BET is one
of the many companies that has exchanged a colourful, if
obsolete name (The British Electric Traction Company) for a
set of anonymous initials; added to that, you don't see our
name on all the products on the supermarket shelf. Because
BET isn't a household name, we have had to work harder
than most companies to establish a supportive shareholder
base . . . Why don't all companies go so far as us? Maybe
they've forgotten who actually owns the company or perhaps they don't feel they can justify the cost. It's possible
that some companies don't share our desire for loyalty.
More likely many, if not most, companies have simply not
yet recognised the need to communicate with their owners.
And if they don't keep their shareholders informed, it
might be worth asking whether they take much trouble to
communicate with their employees and customers.' BET
has also gone to considerable lengths to use plain English in
its shareholder circulars, financial reports and so on and
has installed a toll-free telephone line for shareholders
(and employees) to get further information.

Even those that do not go quite as far as BET can still
make an effort to get their shareholders to identify more
closely with the company's products. Allied-Lyons, for
instance, give shareholders a 'menu' for the buffet that
usually follows their AGMs. Everything laid in front of shareholders is an Allied-Lyons product, including the Lyons

Tetley tea, the Harveys Bristol Cream and other sherries, various beers and wines, as well as the Maryland Cookies and Pasticcini biscuits, the cocktail biscuits and even the canapé cases.

Shortly before its takeover by Trusthouse Forte, the restaurant group Kennedy Brookes invited its shareholders to look over its development of the London Pavilion site in Piccadilly Circus. The discomfort of having to wear hard hats while scrambling over a building site was offset to some extent by a slap-up lunch afterwards in a nearby Wheelers Restaurant, part of the chain. Another invitation from a small company to its shareholders came from the steam-driven Bluebell Railway in Sussex. This time it was not hard hats that were the order of the day, but Wellington boots. The chairman suggested that such footwear would be necessary when issuing the invitation to attend the opening of an extension to the line.

However much directors may dislike or despair of AGMs in this country, they should be very thankful that they are not managing a Japanese company instead. Things are very different there indeed. Many AGMs are disrupted by people who can only be described as gangsters. Usually connected with organised crime, these professional shareholders are known as *sokaiya* and will disrupt meetings unless paid off in advance by the company. Since 1982 such pay-offs have been illegal, but the fact that so many *sokaiya* prey on meetings is an indication that it is still a profitable occupation. Meetings can drag on and on as one protester after another makes tedious and lengthy statements, criticising the company about some indiscretion or other, sometimes of a fairly trivial nature. Japan being what it is, having dirty linen washed in public is considered a loss of face and companies will go to considerable lengths to try to avoid it.

Those Western financial groups operating in the Far East have a good deal more than the gyrations of the markets to contend with. Capel-Cure Myers took great care, when planning its Hong Kong offices, to ensure that they met with the approval of the Fung Shui man. He is brought in to check the relationship of elements such as earth and water in every building there, charging by the square foot for his services. (It was one such chap who forced the Hongkong and Shanghai Bank to move the lions in front of their massive new HQ because they were at an unlucky angle.)

The Fung Shui hurdle was surmounted but, after a while, the capital markets operations suddenly began making heavy losses, inexplicable to the Western bosses. They expressed their puzzlement to the locals. 'What do you expect?' they were asked. 'Two of the office goldfish died last week.'

The goldfish were replaced and, almost immediately, the department returned to profit. Great care is now taken by the mystified Occidentals of all office wildlife and vegetation.

The *sokaiya* turned up at the first annual meeting of NTT, the recently-privatised telecommunications giant and the world's biggest private company (NTT is worth more than the whole Frankfurt and Hong Kong stock exchanges combined). After the *sokaiya* began their questioning, a group of substantially-built gentlemen began to close in on them, persuading them that it might be more tactful simply to leave the hall. It was not clear whether they were members of the police or muscle power hired by the company.

The threat of *sokaiya* is still very real in Japan. Because of it 1,300 companies all held their AGMs on the very same day in 1988 to try to thin the numbers out at each meeting. Presumably it thinned out the numbers of shareholders as well. Half the meetings were attended by plain-clothes police, with 2,300 of them deployed that day. The headquarters of one bank, being investigated by the Finance Ministry for unauthorised lending, was even surrounded by riot police to prevent trouble from the *sokaiya*! British directors should consider themselves fortunate indeed.

One company that appeals for its shareholders to attend the AGM is Berkshire Hathaway, which we have met earlier in this book. Writing in his 1987 Annual Report (you should recall from earlier that Mrs B runs the Furniture Mart), chairman Warren Buffett says that 'Last year we again had about 450 shareholders at our annual meeting. The 60 or so questions they asked were, as always, excellent. At many companies, the annual meeting is a waste of time because exhibitionists turn it into a sideshow. Ours, however, is different. It is informative for shareholders and fun for us. (At Berkshire's meetings, the exhibitionists are on the dais.)

'This year our meeting will be on May 23, 1988 in Omaha, and we hope that you come. The meeting provides the forum for you to ask any owner-related questions you may have, and we will keep answering until all (except those dealing with portfolio activities or other proprietary information) have been dealt with.

'Last year we rented two buses – for $100 – to take shareholders interested in the trip to the Furniture Mart. Your actions demonstrated your good judgment: You snapped up about $40,000 of bargains. Mrs B regards this expense/sales ratio as on the high side and attributes it to my chronic inattention to costs and generally sloppy managerial practices. But, gracious as always, she has offered me another chance and we will again have buses available following the meeting. Mrs B says you must beat last year's sales figures, and I have told her she won't be disappointed.'

Let it not be thought that, here in the UK, companies let shareholders get to their feet and spout off, without listening to a word they say. TSB's first AGM since floating on the stock market, in 1987, was held on a Friday. 'Did the board not realise,' said one of the more elderly share-holders present, 'that British Rail's Senior Citizen Railcard was not valid on Fridays?'

The following year's AGM was held on a Thursday instead!

10

Institutional Madness

If the attention which companies pay to their private investors can be somewhat wanting, that could hardly be said of their sycophantic attitude towards their institutional shareholders. Perhaps it is not too surprising that even the most domineering of directors become servile lickspittles in the presence of fund managers when you consider just how powerful these people really are. The vast majority of pension funds in Britain are run by only a handful of specialist fund management groups. Many of the largest companies in the country are, in effect, controlled by a mere half dozen of these outfits for, although individual funds may have different managers, when it comes to making the really important decisions management houses are likely to act as one. Decisions by only six such houses may decide the entire future of a company.

It is because of the institutionalisation of our savings (about which, you may have gathered, I am not overhappy) that the fate of companies can be decided in the time it takes an eye to twinkle. Although there are cases where, in an evenly balanced fight, the decisions of individuals can still affect the outcome, this is relatively rare. I wonder why companies are so keen on their institutional shareholders when all the evidence points to them being over-concerned with the short-term and incredibly disloyal, even to those companies which have spent a great deal of time and effort on investor relations.

Private investors, on the other hand, tend to be tenaciously loyal, particularly when their board have their backs to the wall. Much of this loyalty may be due to inertia (to accept a takeover bid you have to go to the considerable effort of filling in a form – far easier to do nothing), but it also seems that individual investors are more readily prepared to give their directors the benefit of the doubt and hand them another chance.

The liabilities of the insurance companies and, to an even greater extent, the pension funds, stretch out for a generation or more ahead. If anyone needs to concentrate on the longer-term investment picture, it is these august bodies. Their behaviour on the morning of the 13th April 1988 is an excellent illustration of the responsible attitude taken by the insitutions. At around eight-thirty, phones throughout the City suddenly began ringing. Warburgs were on the blower, offering 630 pence for shares in Rowntree on behalf of the Swiss confectionery giant Suchard. Did the fund managers pause to ask themselves why Suchard might be offering 630 pence when the price of Rowntree up till that moment had been just 480 pence? Did they consider whether this might be the prelude to a full bid? Did they need time to weigh up the pros and cons? Did they consider whether Rowntree's management should be given the chance to put its side of the argument? Did they reflect upon the widely held belief that it is usually wrong to sell out in a dawn raid?

Unfortunately for Rowntree, too few of them did any of

In 1987 the shares of a computer products company, Quest Group, leapt 28 pence in less than an hour. The cause? An announcement on the Stock Exchange's Topic screens said that the company had won an order worth £40 million from the Soviet Union for electronic conveyor belting machinery, an order which would add 40% to the company's net asset value.

The only problem was that it hadn't. Quest's stockbrokers quickly got onto the Exchange to point out that the thing must be a hoax and the shares were suspended. The announcement emanated from a public telex office where, to conceal their identity, the culprit had used a phone card.

About 50 trades were carried out in the hour before the hoax was discovered and, although the Exchange cancelled all the bargains done in that time, the culprit was never discovered!

Such hoaxes have occurred throughout the Stock Exchange's history. 'Chronicles and Characters of the Stock Exchange,' published in the middle of the nineteenth century, records an attempt to rig the market in Government stocks in Queen Anne's reign.

'Passing the Queen's Road, riding at a furious rate, ordering turnpikes to be thrown open and loudly proclaiming the sudden death of the Queen, rode a well-dressed man, sparing neither spur nor steed. From west to east, and from north to south, the news spread. Like wildfire it passed through the deserted fields where villas now abound till it reached the city. The train bands desisted from their exercise, furled their colours, and returned home with their arms reserved. The funds fell with a suddenness which marked the importance of the intelligence . . .'

those things. It took less than half an hour for Suchard to mop up 12% of the shares in one of Britain's biggest companies, taking its stake to 14.9%.

It must be wonderful to be as decisive as the fund managers who sold out that morning on the strength of just one phone call. Presumably their razor-sharp minds convinced them that an overnight profit of 35% was sufficient reward for having bought the shares in the first place and they felt no qualms when City analysts began, only later that day, talking of the possibility of a fight for control of the company at a sharply higher price. They would not, presumably, have been overly concerned that the shares rose another 100 pence in the following fortnight or that the rival confectionery giant Nestlé made its first bid for Rowntree at 890 pence. The 950 pence offered by Suchard in its retaliatory offer will have left them unmoved, while they no doubt laughed off the £10.75 final offer by Nestlé, the level at which the Rowntree board finally capitulated and 71% more than they had got for their shares only two months earlier.

If I had been granted three wishes at that time, I think one would have been to be a fly on the wall when those fund managers next met their trustees and had to explain their actions. That would have been something. (A second would have been that I had had the nerve to hold on to my Rowntree shares until the battle had run its course, rather than sell them a couple of weeks earlier. The third would, of course, have been to have had more Rowntree shares than I actually did have!)

There has been considerable discussion about whether the various financial institutions take a short-term attitude towards investment. The discussion boils down to this: companies say the institutions are concerned overwhelmingly with the short-term, the institutions say they are not. The argument runs: 'You are.' 'We're not.' 'Oh, yes you are.' 'Oh, no we're not.' Instead of everybody joining in, however, as in all the best pantomimes, the two sides then get bored and leave the problem, if there is one, to simmer along quietly until another Rowntree rears its head.

The Bank of England has researched into the question of the City and short-termism, finding that, on the whole, most institutions are not tempted by the chance of a short-term gain in a takeover battle. Surely having the Bank question fund managers about their mental attitudes is much like a headmaster questioning his pupils: Do they like school? Do they do their homework conscientiously? Do they smoke or drink? Do they want to grow up into citizens worthy of the community? We would know all the answers before the questions were even asked, but that does not mean that we are necessarily so gullible as to believe them.

There is plenty of evidence to confirm one in the view that the City is indeed becoming more short-termist in outlook. In the 70s, it was usual for a pension fund to hold an investment in a UK company for an average of 16 years. By 1981, according to figures from the very same Bank of England, that period had halved to eight years. In 1987, the average share was held for a mere two years. So over half a pension fund's portfolio is now turned over in just one year. Over half. How can managers possibly argue that they are investing for future generations when they are presented with startling figures like that? The insurance companies also now turn over half their portfolios each year, while the investment trusts manage a 90% turnover rate. Even that palls beside the unit trust groups which, in 1987, managed to achieve a record turnover rate of over 140%, churning their entire portfolios of UK shares every nine months!

There might possibly be some justification for this frenzied activity if it led directly to a superior performance by the funds, but that doesn't seem to be the case. UK pension funds have underperformed all the relevant stock market indices over the past five years. In 1987, the stock market here returned 8%, but the average pension fund's

The reactions of investors to the Crash of '87 varied, and were undoubtedly most severe in the United States.

There, Dr Grover Philippi dressed up in a Santa Claus outfit and, furious with his stockbroker for losing his life savings, kidnapped him from a Christmas party. He took him to a cabin near the West Virginia border and tortured him for two weeks with a homemade electric chair and a cattle prod.

Stories of the behaviour of stockbrokers dismissed on both sides of the Atlantic became legion, but also infuriatingly difficult to substantiate. One in London, on hearing that he had been sacked, is said to have made a bonfire of his papers on his office desk before leaving. Another is said to have used his, or rather the firm's car, as a battering ram to inflict his displeasure on the other cars in the car park. Another is claimed to have parked his Porsche outside his erstwhile office, turned on the stereo full blast, switched on all the electrical equipment, locked it and then thrown the keys down a drain!

return was just 7.1%. Bank of England figures show that many funds had invested very heavily in equities in 1987 and were still buying them hand over fist when the Crash came. Like so many sheep, they then all panicked into cash and then, in the first quarter of 1988, into government securities just as interest rates began picking up again. And even on those occasions when their strategic decisions are correct, dealing costs and spreads are obviously going to eat far more severely into the portfolio of a fund that deals furiously than a more passive one.

Fund managers taken to task for adopting short-term attitudes blame the fact that they have to report to their trustees every three months. Portfolio measurement is these days quite an exact science and it is all too easy for trustees to compare their performance with other funds and pick fault with a manager who has done poorly. For a pension fund with liabilities stretching decades ahead, it is ludicrous to be judged on how well it does over just three months. It is as if a marathon, instead of being run as a whole, was organised instead as a series of hundred yard dashes. Yet fund management groups fight tooth and nail for the right to look after pension fund money, not altogether surprising when you consider that they are paid £500 million each year. The constant fear of dismissal hanging over them means that many fund managers cannot afford to take a contrary investment view which may take several years to come right. Instead, they find themselves compelled to follow the herd, even though this route leads to mediocrity or even worse.

The threat of dismissal is not an idle one either, although managers were probably safer while stock markets always seemed to be rising. One of the more widely-publicised dismissals came in July 1988 when British Rail's pension fund, the fifth biggest in Britain, sacked one of their six investment management companies less than two years after appointing them. Because of the time taken to arrange the fund, the company was in fact given only a year before being given the boot. Its crime? To produce a return just 1.3% below the middle-ranked fund for the year to April 1988. Averages being what they are, half the funds are obviously going to under-perform. How can managers possibly manage if a ranking in the bottom half brings down the sword of Damocles hanging over their head? If trustees decide on the basis of just a few quarters' figures to switch investment managers, the pension fund world will soon be in absolute chaos. Yet that appears to be the way things are heading.

Faced with the inability to out-perform, an increasing number of fund managers are striving instead simply to match the performance of the various stock indices. The indexing of funds is very popular in the United States and, like so many investment ideas, is becoming more firmly rooted over here. Funds will invest in stocks that can be expected to track the various indices with only a small variation. This investment method is also called passive fund management and, although this sounds as though there is nothing for the manager to do, it is a surprisingly sophisticated technique requiring the use of computers. The fact that passive fund managers charge less for their services than the chaps who claim to be able to beat the indices by wheeling and dealing (around a third of their fees) will no doubt make this method more and more attractive to trustees.

> You should not necessarily be depressed if your portfolio slightly underperforms the market as a whole. Tax reformer and wider share ownership campaigner Philip Chappell explains it with his Sigma Factor: 'It is a statistical certainty that the sum of investors will under-perform the sum of investment indices by the amount of stamp duty, commission, management charges et cetera.'

Portfolio management techniques in the United States are streets ahead of us, if you measure these things by their complexity. There is little sign of their funds being any more successful than ours at beating the indices but they try. Oh boy, how they try. Stanislas Yassukovich is one of the more erudite of the Square Mile's leading lights. One-time deputy chairman of the Stock Exchange and chairman of The Securities Association, he was also a leading light in Merrill Lynch, the US stockbroking firm that claims to have 'brought Wall Street to Main Street' and has seen investment life on both sides of the Atlantic. A big campaign by the Stock Exchange there in the 50s and 60s to bring individuals into the stock market worked magnificently but 'The process which leads inexorably to the decline of the individual saver as a direct participant in the equity market can be described as a vicious circle. The collective investment schemes, whether they be those directly soliciting funds from individual savers such as unit trusts, or those passively collecting savings such as pension funds, are subject to competitive pressures like any other participant in the economic system.

'Those competitive pressures have intensified in recent years due to an increase in the availability of statistical information allowing for a more precise and detailed analysis of competitive investment performance. Whereas the pitch was "give me your savings to manage – I performed better than my competitors during the last twelve months", in the United States the pitch is now "I performed better than my competitors last week".

'As the period of measurement for comparative investment performance shortens, those responsible for managing collective investment schemes seek methods of ensuring better short term performance. These include use of derivative products and computerised techniques such as program trading and so-called portfolio insurance. These techniques and the consequent complexity in market activity serve to drive the individual investor away from direct participation and into collective investment schemes.

'The individual considers himself ill-equipped to cope with these complexities of the market, having neither the time nor the computer power nor the access to professional dealing facilities to cope on his own. He becomes resigned, therefore, to handing over whatever portion of his savings he felt capable of investing directly to the unit trust or mutual fund, thereby completing the circle, since in

[187]

choosing *which* unit trust he will, of course, be heavily influenced by the short term comparative statistics made available to him. This competitive process has given birth to the ugly phrase "short-termism" but those who most complain of its negative consequences are themselves caught up in the competitive nature of investment management. It is now a common experience to hear the same company chairman who complains bitterly of volatility in his company's share price and the lack of loyalty demonstrated by institutions when a predator is on the prowl coolly remarking that he recently changed his pension fund manager because of inadequate performance during the last quarter.'

Although the world stock market crash of October 1987 received quite heavy coverage in the UK media, none went quite so far as one New York tabloid. Its front page consisted of only two words. In bold black type inches high it read: **BLOOD BATH.**

Some of the methods American institutions used are believed by many to have worsened the Crash of October 1987 and to have increased the volatility of the stock market. As I mentioned earlier, Warren Buffett is one fund manager who does not believe in the need to watch the stock market like a hawk. He doesn't even have machines in his office to give him current share prices. He is less than flattering about many of his peers, however. 'In October the market experienced a sudden, massive seizure. We have "professional" investors, those who manage many billions, to thank for most of this turmoil. Instead of focusing on what businesses will do in the years ahead, many prestigious money managers now focus on what they expect other money managers to do in the days ahead. For them, stocks are merely tokens in a game, like the thimble and flatiron in Monopoly.

'An extreme example of what their attitude leads to is "portfolio insurance," a money-management strategy that many leading investment advisors embraced in 1986–1987. This strategy – which is simply an exotically-labelled version of the small speculator's stop-loss order – dictates that ever-increasing portions of a stock portfolio, or their index-future equivalents, be sold as prices decline. The strategy says nothing else matters. A Downtick of a given magnitude automatically produces a huge sell order. According to the Brady Report, $60 billion to $90 billion of equities were poised on this hair trigger in mid-October of 1987.

'If you've thought that investment advisors were hired to invest, you may be bewildered by this technique . . . Would you sell your house to whatever bidder was available at 9:31 on some morning merely because at 9:30 a similar house sold for less than it would have brought on the previous day?

'Moves like that, however, are what portfolio insurance tells a pension fund or university to make when it owns a portion of enterprises such as Ford or General Electric. The less these companies are being valued at, says this approach, the more vigorously they should be sold. As a "logical" corollary, the approach commands the institutions to repurchase these companies – *I'm not making this up* – once their prices have rebounded significantly. Considering that huge sums are controlled by managers following such Alice-in-Wonderland practices, is it any surprise that markets sometimes behave in aberrational fashion?'

A small positive sign is the decision by one large group,

Henderson Pension Fund Management, to cease giving quarterly performance figures to its clients, instead concentrating on a rolling 12-month appraisal in an effort to cure the 'plague of short-termism'.

As long ago as 1935, John Maynard Keynes said 'Professional investors are concerned not with making superior long-term forecasts of the probable yield of an investment over its whole life but with foreseeing changes in the conventional basis of valuation a short time ahead of the general public. They are concerned not with what an investment is really worth to a man who buys it for keeps, but with what the market will value it at, under the influence of mass psychology, three months or a year hence.'

That short-termist attitudes are prevalent is surely without doubt. Where they lay the blame for them is a much more difficult matter. Fund managers blame the companies and their trustees. The companies blame the fund managers. When the CBI surveyed its members' attitudes on this subject, they asked 200 companies what might prevent them from making investments which they believed would be in the long-term interests of their business. 12% claimed that a fear of takeover was 'of major significance,' 23% highlighted pressure from financial institutions while 41% believed that their share price might suffer as a result.

Even if short-term attitudes are *not* held by the City's institutions, the belief among companies that they are is influencing their behaviour. Sir Hector Laing of United Biscuits went on record in the midst of the battle for Rowntree to accuse large investors of acting like prostitutes, selling a company's shares at the first sound of a takeover bid. He went further, accusing some stockbrokers and merchant bankers of touting for business by initiating bids.

With such views widespread among companies, even if not so forcefully expressed, it is not surprising that instead

of running their businesses in the way that they think best for the long-term future of the company, directors instead feel compelled to produce rabbits out of the hat every so often just to keep their institutional shareholders happy. As a result, necessary investment that may take time to bear fruit may be shelved. Why should a fund manager use his fund to support a company that has just committed itself to a ten year programme of investment in research and development, or to a new factory or something similar, if he fears he is not going to be managing those funds when those plans come to fruition? Why would a company's board sanction a project that may bring great rewards in several years time but which may, because it reduces profits in the short-term, harm the price of their shares? With the threat of takeover in the back of the mind of practically every director in the country, a share price is something to be constantly massaged upwards, not allowed to fall. (The detrimental effect on their share options is purely incidental, of course).

The problem of short-termism is a very real one, as even the Chancellor realises. When discussing the ludicrous Personal Equity Plans Mr Lawson said he hoped (forlornly, as I told him at the time. But does he ever listen to me?) that they would help 'to reverse the long-term trend to institutional ownership of British industry. This is desirable for two reasons: first, the widespread ownership of shares will cement the identity between the interests of the corporate sector and the population as a whole; and second, the individual shareholder's attitude to his investment is quite distinct from that of the institution, which is increasingly under pressure to achieve superior investment performance over very short periods.

'A better mixture between individual and institutional shareholders might enable companies to plan investment and research and development for the longer term rather than being pressed to achieve profits in the short term.'

He has been quoted in the *Financial Times* as saying that private shareholders, if treated well, could help rid companies of some of the pressures to produce short-term results, 'because I think that if there are short-term operators they tend to be the financial institutions – ironically, the pension funds.'

Bob Stovall, the American stockbroking guru who appears elsewhere in this book, has two business cards. The smaller measures only two inches by one inch and reads (if you look closely enough):

THE LACK OF ORDERS
FROM YOU HAS MADE
THIS ECONOMY SIZE CARD
NECESSARY

On the other side is printed:

I AM AN IMPORTANT
CATHOLIC.
IN CASE OF AN ACCIDENT
PLEASE NOTIFY A BISHOP.

If the government realises that this problem exists and is so serious, and if (as it says) it is so keen on spreading share ownership among individuals rather than institutions, why has it not done anything concrete to turn the tide? Not only has the tide not been turned, but the institutions now own a greater proportion of UK company shares than they did before the privatisation programme started. As Lord Vinson has said: 'It happened inadvertently, it was not premeditated and the consequences were unforeseen – but giving pension funds tax exempt status had led to the greatest shift of ownership from individuals to institutions since the opposite happened at the time of the Dissolution of the Monasteries. And the process is accelerating. Yet it runs clean contrary to a fundamental principle of Tory philosophy, namely that the diffusion of economic power, and the multiple sources of patronage which flow from it, are prerequisites of a free society. The process must be reversed before it is too late.'

So the Chancellor believes the institutions are guilty of short-termism. The Stock Exchange believes the institutions are guilty of short-termism. The Confederation of British Industry believes that institutions are guilty of short-termism. Many companies believe the institutions are guilty of short-termism. Even some fund managers believe that they are forced by the system into the crime of short-termism. Yet no-one is prepared to try to tackle the problem. Indeed it is arguable that no particular group acting on its own could tackle it, particularly as this seems to be very much a worldwide problem.

When Chancellor, Nigel Lawson said that it is not a matter for legislation, but that it is up to the Stock Exchange to take the initiative. As far as I can see, the government, and only the government, can solve this. Pension funds are given tax exemption. Instead of being a virtual *carte blanche* exemption, there should be tighter rules. How about starting, for instance, by making the sale of any share within a year of its purchase liable to Capital Gains Tax? I would have thought that would help apply the brake to some of the more outrageous speculative activity by the pension funds.

11

The Insiders

Is there anything more infuriating than reading in the papers that one of your companies has just produced fantastic results, only to discover that the shares have fallen back because the City was 'disappointed' with them or because the profits were 'below expectations'? There are now few companies on the stock market that aren't researched by somebody or other. The biggest firms may have a score or more analysts scribbling away writing research notes which then get circulated to the firm's clients, most of whom will then shove them straight into the bin. One fund manager told me that in his office there is a giant waste-paper basket on wheels into which he and his colleagues tip the vast majority of the mountain of paper that arrives from stockbrokers every day.

Where do the analysts get their figures from in the first place? It would be nice to believe that they have no greater facilities at their disposal than you or I and merely derive their weighty conclusions from long hours poring over the company's Annual Report with their calculators, perhaps looking at a few trade papers and popping out occasionally

Those who believe that economists have no real value at all ('Economists have successfully predicted 14 of the last 5 recessions,' said David Fehr) may be encouraged in their views by the caveat that appears at the front of the Reviews produced by the National Institute of Economic and Social Research.

'This Review is intended to be of service to those, in business and elsewhere, who need to take a view of the general economic situation and prospects. The workings of the economy are not fully understood; and even if they were economic prediction would remain hazardous because of the impact of political events and technological developments. Nevertheless, the Institute believes that a group of economists, presenting a comprehensive account of current economic developments and a coherent view of likely trends, can perform a useful service.'

to the High Street or the supermarket to see how the company's products are selling. Such thoughts would be very wide of the mark, of course, for stockbrokers' analysts have access to the most useful source of information of all, one that is denied to we lesser mortals – the companies themselves.

Much of an analyst's work involves visiting the various businesses in his sector, talking to the management and examining its operations at first hand. He, or she, will try to cultivate the friendship or acquaintance of the more important officers of the company. If some important news breaks, they want to be one whose phone calls the company returns first. When they meet the management they may, through a process that owes more to the era of nods and winks than the computer age, hint at their forecasts for profits and, if they are lucky, the managing director or finance director may indicate whether he considers this about right, or whether he feels it may be on the low or the

high side. Even if he does not go that far, he might still let the analyst know where his forecast stands in relation to his peers at rival stockbroking firms, implying which of the other analysts he considers to be good at their jobs.

Some analysts actually let the company get a glimpse of what they are writing before it is sent out. If the company wants to keep the goodwill of the analyst's firm, it is likely to point out anything particularly untoward that might leave the analyst with egg on his face if it is published unaltered.

Even though the stockbrokers know the vast majority of what they produce is never read, it does not stop them churning out ever more paper. The human race needs trees to survive. Stockbrokers need to chop them down to survive. If the institutional clients do not deal, how can the brokers pay for their expensive staff, computers and offices? One of the best ways of persuading them to deal is to put out a 'buy' or a 'sell' circular on a particular company and then have their salesmen ring up and badger the fund managers until one or two of them cave in just to get a bit of peace and quiet.

One of the problems with all this is that if your analyst produces a circular which forecasts a company's profits in the coming year or two pretty much in line with every other stockbroker in the country, it is unlikely that you are going to get very much business as a result. Far better if an analyst sticks his neck out and estimates profits higher than all the others are going for, particularly if he has a good reputation. Then the salesman stands more of a chance of getting some business on the back of it. Of course, another analyst may spoil this by producing a profits forecast that is even higher, only to be followed by another and yet another. It does not take too much imagination to see that before long the forecasts will be wildly out of touch with reality. Come the actual results, significantly below the consensus in the City, and it is understandable that there might be room for 'disappointment' amongst the funds that have bought the shares even if, to the layman sitting at home reading his paper, the figures on their own look quite splendid.

It isn't only through the brokers' circulars that this game is played. There are plenty of examples in the stock market reports of share prices moving after another infamous 'broker's lunch' where a select gathering of fund managers are invited in to the stockbroker's offices to meet representatives of a company. Should anything interesting crop up as the port is being passed around, then it usually isn't too long before the share price moves with, as thanks for arranging the lunch, the business being transacted with the host broker.

Companies will frequently arrange big briefings with analysts and fund managers themselves. In June 1988, for

---

The *Sun* is not renowned for its financial journalism, but this editorial deserves to go down in the annals:

SLICK AS THIEVES

Strange tales, or rather bad smells, are emerging from the City.

There is more blatant hanky-panky going on in the financial world than for a long time and the City is turning a blind eye.

The sharks gloat openly as they flout the gentlemanly rules of big business. They know that the risk of being jailed is infinitely smaller than that of the humble shoplifter.

Nothing would do more to dispel the idea that the Government cares only about the rich than for it to come down like a ton of hot bricks on those City slickers who engage so profitably in legalised robbery.

instance, Hanson invited about a hundred analysts and fund managers to an all-day symposium with Lord Hanson and Sir Gordon White, as well as various other executives from the Hanson group. The lunchtime speaker was the American politician Walter Mondale.

A five nation tour was recently laid on of various parts of the Allied-Lyons empire, taking in the United States, Canada and France for 90 assorted fund managers, analysts and journalists. Such exalted personalities could hardly expect anything less than the best, so a Concorde was used to shuttle them about. As one brewery analyst remarked to me at the time, it made a change from the previous year when there had been a tour round three of Allied's plants in the UK in an ageing Viscount! A spokeman for the company responded to the criticism of the expense of this jaunt, believed to be almost a million pounds, by claiming that if the company succeeded in getting its message across, the tour could pay for itself. Even a ha'penny on the share price would add £3.5 million to the group's market value, he said. In the week the partying was going on, the shares lost 22 pence, wiping £157 million off Allied's capitalisation! Although the majority of those on the trip were happy enough to accept the company's hospitality, one or two stockbroking firms had sufficient scruples to insist on paying for their analysts to attend.

Perhaps private investors don't mind the kid glove treatment given to the institutions? Perhaps they don't mind that they receive a completely different treatment to the fund managers, simply because they hold a small number of shares? It is surprising that so much of this company-City contact is permitted. Why do shares rise so often after brokers' lunches, for instance, or after company briefings? Has some price-sensitive gossip been vouchsafed to the favoured few? If so, is that not passing on inside information? If not, why are the analysts and fund managers so very keen to attend these sorts of events? Companies are supposed to release price-sensitive information to everybody at one and the same time, not leak it out in dribs and drabs, beginning with those they consider most important. Dealing on inside information, if it is such, is now supposed to be illegal in Britain and a prison sentence can result for somebody guilty of the offence.

Not every country regards insider trading with the distaste it now properly seems to arouse in Britain (Sir Martin Jacomb must rue the day he called it 'a victimless crime'). In New Zealand, insider trading is not only legal but is practically encouraged. There is even an association, the Society for the Promotion of Insider Trading run by Steve Spelman.

Subscribers pay £150 a year for the Insider Trading Hotline and are then telephoned with inside information. Spelman gets this by advertising for informants. Anyone giving information leading to a rise of a fifth in the value of the particular share in the following two months receives £400, with the payout increasing for larger movements than that.

It is not difficult to understand why companies take part in this game. It is, after all, in their interests to make sure that their business is well understood in the City and that their shares are 'fairly valued.' Companies that don't play along may find their share prices suffering as a result, leading to the fear, or even the dread reality of a takeover. If the business is going to be analysed anyway, isn't it better to make sure that the analysis is as accurate as possible?

Yet failure to achieve the often hyped-up consensus City forecast can be disastrous. A few years ago Hawker Sid-

[201]

deley's results shocked the City, which had been ludicrously over-optimistic in its estimates of the company's profits. When they were announced, the share price plunged. Analysts across the Square Mile were furious that they had been misled by the company. In fact Hawker Siddeley had merely been more honourable than many other companies, believing that price sensitive information should be released simultaneously, so avoiding any help or hints for the analysts with their forecasts. Its image in the City, however, suffered as a result.

Hawker's is not alone. Other companies have decided that they don't want to play the game any more. GKN gave up analysts' lunches in 1987. In June 1988 Scottish and Newcastle Breweries decided they were fed up with City speculation about a takeover bid and cancelled all briefings with analysts. The chief executive, Alick Rankin, believed that the background briefings were merely being used by brokers to drum up business. 'The City has become a place of desperation, with jockeying for position with information. We seem to be treated like casino chips. As far as the City is concerned we are just a set of initials.

'The scene in the City has changed. It doesn't seem to matter whether the share price movement is bogus and speculative. There are people in the market who want a bid to happen – the people have helped to create the heightened excitement. They are using S&N as a means of recouping their losses of last October.' The bid came just months later.

There are some sceptics who say that the whole process has now gone so far that the City is not only forecasting company results, but actually influencing them. The fear of 'disappointing' analysts may lead companies to indulge in window-dressing or creative accounting in order to bring the numbers closer into line with the predictions!

Writing shortly after the stock market crash in 1987, when analysts had suddenly – and belatedly – moved from being bullish to being very pessimistic, the vice chairman of the General Electric Company, Ronald Grierson, said: 'When most businesses were privately owned, proprietors tightened their belts in lean years and sat things out. Public corporations living in goldfish bowls somehow find this humiliating and resort to financial acrobatics to maintain the dynamic of growth . . . all cannot be well with the integrity of investment analysis when shares are a 'buy' one day at a vast multiple of earnings, yet are rejected as unattractive three weeks later when all that has changed is that they have become cheaper. What is being analysed is the anticipated short-term behaviour of other investors, not the intrinsic soundness of the business.'

Even when it turns sour, the generally cosy relationship between companies and the City is unlikely to disappear overnight. Stockbrokers and institutional investors will continue to be privy to information that reaches the ears of lesser shareholders and investors only some time afterwards. Although it is possible to argue that much of it is inside information, it seems to be the accepted way of doing things and one can hardly imagine an analyst, fund manager or finance director hurled into the chokey simply for doing what they see to be their job.

Even without this relationship, the access of the financial professionals to sophisticated electronic information services will always give them the jump on us, although innovations like the Stock Exchange's Market-Eye may be closing the gap slightly. One should not assume, however, that the access to all this information makes the professionals any better at investment than we are. They are frequently unable to see the wood for the trees (those that have not been cut down to turn into brokers' circulars).

Share tipsters tend to have very short memories, pointing to their successes proudly while discovering they have terrible lapses of memory when it comes to recalling their less triumphant recommendations.

In its *Private Client Newsbrief*, which usually tells it like it is, Capel-Cure Myers came clean and admitted that the Japanese bonds they had recommended had not done particularly well, following an unexpected hike in interest rates by the Japanese authorities.

'Because of the general confusion that seems to be prevalent at the moment, it is probably right to drop back into the foxhole and simply give the muffled comment that we are fairly unenthusiastic about the short-term outlook for most markets, with the exception of Hong Kong.'

It then added: 'Probably as this goes to print, forty-eight million crack Chinese troops are dancing around the smoking remains of the Governor-General's house.'

Take Rowntree, for instance. There had been an enormous amount of publicity about the benefits to flow through from 1992 and the importance of companies thinking in pan-European terms long before the bid turned up, with various entrepreneurs taking advantage of the DTI's generous offer of free publicity to plug the campaign and themselves.

Yet barely a whisper was heard in the City about the effects of all this. The importance of internationally-known brands such as Smarties, Rolo and Kit Kat was barely considered. Then, overnight, it all changed when Suchard bought Rowntree's shares in the dawn raid. From having been fairly lukewarm about Rowntree shares, all the analysts were suddenly unanimously aware of the attractions of its brands which had been there all the while. These highly paid, highly intellectual, highly ridiculous people all sagely agreed that there now had to be a bid for Rowntree. It stood to reason. Just think of all those brands, known throughout Europe. Come to think of it. What about all the other companies with well-known brand names? Suddenly brands were the thing. Analysts who had hitherto ignored the goodwill value of the products made by the companies in their sectors had to invent some way of valuing them.

Another well-publicised instance of City professionals failing to appreciate the real worth of a company came when Racal announced that it planned to float off its Vodafone subsidiary. The announcement sent the share price of Racal soaring from £1.5bn to £2bn within a matter of a few hours. Within a few months, it was clear that Vodafone itself might be worth around £2 billion, over half a billion pounds more than the stock market had valued the entire company only a few months earlier. If the subsidiary was worth so much on the open market, why had it been valued so poorly before that? It doesn't make sense.

It took the interest of two Swiss companies to open the City's eyes to the value of brands, two companies who knew that they were worth a great deal more than the City had hitherto been valuing them at. It took Racal's announcement of the flotation of Vodafone to waken the analysts to the true value of the company as a whole. All the whizzy electronic equipment in the world won't give the City an advantage if analysts can't see further than the ends of their noses. All that contact with companies won't benefit them if they don't listen to what they are being told. And, while most analysts are very good at juggling with numbers, very few have any first-hand experience of the businesses on which they sit in judgement. One can well understand the irritation of leading businessmen with the spotty analysts, often in their twenties, perhaps just out of college, who try telling them how to run their companies. Sad to say, I have yet to hear of any being boxed soundly around the ear, told not to be so cheeky and sent home to mother. Not even Alan Sugar has gone so far yet.

No matter how widely share ownership may be spread, there will always be two classes of investors. Them and Us, the big and the small. It is a pity that a greater number of companies don't realise that the closer the relationship between them and the City, the more short-term expectations may be raised and the more harmful the effects of 'disappointing' those expectations may be. Why companies don't instead concentrate their attention on their private investors, rather than pander to the influence of disloyal institutions, is beyond me. If they grumble continuously about the behaviour of the City, they have only themselves to blame.

I find it rather satisfying, however, to think that despite all the inside information the institutions are privy to, despite all the advice they receive from their stockbrokers, despite their ability to spend their entire working lives studying investment, the majority still underperform the market.

12

The Other Side of the Coin

It is said that in late 1987 there was one list the junk mailers wanted to get their hands on more than any other. It contained just over a quarter of a million names and addresses. They were the people who, despite the stock market Crash, had still gone ahead and applied for shares in British Petroleum. The attractions of the shares (the issue's success was deemed to be a foregone conclusion by everyone) suddenly evaporated as stock markets around the world crumbled. The BP sale was a washout.

Yet, amazingly, on the last day for applications in BP, the television news showed people eagerly handing in their forms. It wasn't even as if this was a completely new issue. BP's existing shares were already traded on the stock market. These individuals were asked whether they did not realise that the shares they were buying for 120 pence each could be bought for just 70 pence on the stock market. Some actually admitted they did, but that they preferred to buy them this way, some seemed to think that the Government would see them alright no matter what the stock market did and some quite obviously didn't know what on earth all the

An ad appeared in 1987 for the Coldwater Investment Group, promoting their New First Arctic Smaller Companies Trust: 'If you have only thought of the Arctic as a vast frozen region some-where north-west of Scotland – the kind of place where the only flotations are ships and icebergs. Think again!

'The Arctic possesses one of the most undervalued fish markets in the world. In addition, small pockets of entrepreneurs look set to net record profits. Take Sven Svenson fish food manufacturers par excellence – since going public last year the company have achieved a 20 point increase on the much revered FFI (Frozen Fish Index) – an enviable achievement.

'So get a slice of the fish cake now. Move in before the clever money does. Simply make your cheque payable to Coldwater Investment Group and leave it in a brown paper bag in the rubbish bin on platform 9, Waterloo Station – don't delay.'

The whole thing was, of course, a spoof, placed by the more normally sedate Scottish Mutual to highlight the marketing zeal of some of its competitors. The way new issues were going at the time, I would not have been surprised if that bin at Waterloo station had not seen a few deposited applications.

reporters were on about, even though the Crash had been the biggest news story for days.

Take the 270,000 people in this great country of ours who decided to throw good money away on BP. If they were such keen bulls of the shares, there was nothing to stop them ringing a stockbroker or marching into their bank and buying the existing shares at the prevailing market price. It is said that the issue's organisers even discovered a handful of multiple applications for BP. They can't have been too difficult to find!

No wonder the junk mailers were so keen to get their claws into these people. If they would pay almost £20 for ten pound notes, what else might they not be persuaded to

buy? Perhaps jointly they might be inveigled into putting in a bid for Tower Bridge or Nelson's Column? If ever you wanted an example to help prove the argument that many of the people caught up in the privatisation bandwagon had not the slightest idea what they were doing, it was surely BP.

I suppose we should be thankful that the Crash took place when it did. What would have happened if the Crash had been just a week later? BP had, after all, been set to draw in more investors than any other share issue in history. If three million people or more had already written out their cheques and posted them when disaster struck the stock market, what on earth would the consquences have been? Investors taking to the barricades? Rioting in the Square Mile? It certainly wouldn't have done the Conservatives' political standing much good.

It would also have been interesting to know what would have transpired had the Crash not materialised at all. BP was, after all, the first privatisation issue of a company which sells to many members of the public and which also faces tough competition doing so. If several million motorists had also been shareholders in BP, what difference would it have made to the battle of the forecourts? I can't believe that the majority of them would not have used BP garages wherever possible, in preference to rival firms. What a stink Shell, Esso, Texaco and the rest would have made then.

I still puzzle over the motives of those BP investors. Perhaps private client stockbrokers are right when they grumble, as they seem frequently to do, that a good many of the investors with whom they have contact are just plain dumb. Unfortunately, there are plenty of instances that would seem to back them up in this.

What, for instance, about the 50,000 people who hadn't

Stockbrokers seem, for some reason, to have got the idea that many of the clients are rather peculiar. One received a letter out of the blue from India.

'Dear Sir,
With due to respect and humbly submission that I would like to receive your monthly review and company research circulars. I collect your address from Investment International monthly magazine. Place me on your mailing list for three months.

Please I request you to send me your monthly magazine, CALENDAR '88, a list of NOBEL PRIZE winners, some INACTIVE postage stamps, a History Book of England, photographs of the Prime Minister Mrs Margaret Thatchar. Must be send above maintioned items.

Yours faithfully . . .'

cashed their British Gas dividend cheques over four months after being sent them? Surely most people know what a cheque looks like these days? Not enough, obviously, to stop a million pounds sloshing around unwanted.

Time after time, calls for the second or third payment on privatised shares have fallen due, only for thousands of investors to have fallen by the wayside. 7,500, for instance, did not pay the second call on their TSB shares, despite innumerable reminders. So they forfeited them, being given back only their original payment of 50 pence and nothing more. Had they not wanted to keep the shares, it would have been far more sensible to have sold them in the market for, at the time, there was a profit of 40 pence on each. The only possible explanation is that those investors did not have the slightest idea of what they were doing. They should never have bought shares in the first place.

Perhaps there ought to be an exam for shareholders, as there is for driving, a similarly dangerous activity. Only those getting above a certain number of the questions right would be permitted to own shares.

The investor who rang up a stockbroker friend of mine shortly after the privatisation of British Aerospace would certainly not have passed. He ordered her to sell his shares at the highest price of the day!

Although Warren Buffett was quoted earlier speaking of the opportunities presented to individual investors when the institutions all rampage in one direction, it isn't only the fund managers who travel in herds. There is a substantial body of private investors who obviously prefer safety in numbers. Nowhere is this clearer than with the tips that appear in the newspapers and newsletters. You would think that the readers of these publications would realise that they are not alone in their literary habits. Not only are there thousands of others reading exactly the same information, but the market makers are also privy to the secret. They aren't in the business to make investors happy. They are there to make money. If a share is tipped, particularly a small company's shares, they will know that the majority of those wanting to deal in its wake will be buyers. The price they made before the tip will obviously not make economic sense afterwards. Instead, they will move it nearer to a level at which buyers and sellers are in equilibrium.

The faith of the public in the abilities of financial journalists verges on the unbelievable at times. A member of the financial team at the independent London radio station, LBC, picked up the phone one day to be asked: 'Excuse me, but can you please tell me what the Pound–German Mark rate will be on September 26th?'

Even if the first few investors manage to deal at a price close to that prevailing when the shares are tipped, the tenth or the hundredth in line are likely to find the shares substantially higher by the time their turn arrives. For years, stockbrokers have grumbled about Monday mornings, when their phones are blazing hot with people wanting to deal on the back of the tips in the Sunday papers, even though most newspapers give no more than two or three lines explaining why they are so keen on the shares (Cynics claim the reason is often that the writer is returning a favour to a market-maker or a public relations chap who needs a puff to get him out of a tricky spot). Thoughts of follow-up research never seem to enter into investors' heads. Indeed, some stockbrokers now open up on Sundays to scoop up some of these orders before investors have a chance to change their minds.

The Stocks and Shares Show provided plenty of examples of the surge in trading encountered by shares that are mentioned publicly. The week before it was tipped, for example, Persimmon saw only 6 trades a day on average in its shares. On the Monday following the Stocks and Shares Show there were 489 trades and another 92 on the Tuesday. There were two trades in Pentos on the Friday before its mention; 489 deals were down on the Monday yet, within a month, the shares had fallen 14%. An average of ten trades a day in Airship Industries zoomed to 528 on the Monday after it was tipped on the Stocks and Shares Show. The shares shot up from 12 pence to 16 pence and were back to 12 again within a week. One market-maker told me how much he liked the programme. He did a third of the business in Airship on that Monday and made £15,000 profit.

Morgan Grenfell looked in detail at the influence of the tips on this programme and concluded, as so many commentators had surmised before them, that 'investors who are thinking of rushing into a share which has been tipped should delay at least a few trading days for the price to settle, and watch out for the influence of long term holders who may be using the tip as an easy selling opportunity. It is rarely worth buying in on the first day after the mention.' They also concluded that fewer than half the shares recommended showed a positive return.

Yet the tipsters continue to exert a powerful influence over the minds of many small investors. Their enthusiasm for one company actually contributed to its collapse. The story of Rotaprint's final months must be one of the most bizarre investment stories of recent years. The company produced printing machines but had fallen on hard times. New management were brought in in 1986 but, although order books were healthy, there were difficulties in producing the firm's new presses.

However, with the shares at just 2.25 pence at the beginning of 1987, Rotaprint attracted the attention of the tipsheets. It became one of the hottest stocks around, rising by over seven hundred per cent to reach 17.5 pence in July. Stockbrokers became so fed up of clients who ignored their warnings about the shares that it became known in the City as 'Rotarubbish'. Investors seemed oblivious to the company's terrible profits record and the lack of an asset backing to the shares.

The board actually went so far as to warn investors that things were getting badly out of hand. At the AGM in July 1987 Chairman John Crates, in a statement that was widely reported, said: 'You must make your own judgement whether a share price of 17-and-a-half pence, which gives a market capitalisation of £77m, reflects the company's present position realistically.' He also pointed out that the board could see no justification to explain the buoyant share price. From that moment on, the share price fell back

[214]

Practically all investment publications publish caveats absolving themselves of any responsibility if things do not happen as they suggest they might. One Japanese tipsheet apparently carries the following warning for its readers: 'The information given here does not represent investment advice. However, we do feel that these reports may be the blood which leads the speculative sharks into a feeding frenzy.'

as the chairman's statement began to sink in. The shares had fallen to 4 pence by end of February 1988 when the receivers were called in.

The tipsheets had dealt not only many investors a bitter blow, but the company as well. In 1986, there were only 2,800 shareholders in Rotaprint. By the time of its collapse, there were over 28,000. The extraordinary dealing activity in the shares cost the company a small fortune. Of its £472,000 loss in the year ending March 1987, around £200,000 was accounted for in registrars' fees alone! Without the enthusiasm of so many investors, the company might even have managed to struggle through.

Although some trade creditors received something from the receivers, there was nothing at all left in the kitty for shareholders. Those still holding shares when the music stopped lost every penny. Despite the warnings from the board, some shareholders felt terribly hard done by and asked the government to investigate the board's handling of the company. Rotaprint must go down in investment history as one of the few companies to be killed by the enthusiasm of investors!

The speculative fever of mid-1987 was a time when rational and traditional investment analysis seemed old hat to many investors. And why not, when worm breeders and schoolboys were apparently investing like Rockefellers. Everyone was brought back to earth again with a bump. Such periods of incredible gains followed by sharp losses have occurred again and again in investment history, with the South Sea bubble probably the best known of all of them. At the time, Edward Harley wrote: 'The demon of stock jobbing is the genius of this place. This fills all hearts, tongues and thoughts, and nothing is to like Bedlam as the present humour, which has seized all parties, Whigs, Tories, Jacobites, Papists and all sects. No one is satisfied with even exhorbitant gains, but everyone thirsts for more, and all this founded upon the machine of paper credit supported by imagination.'

Bernard Baruch's comments made in 1932, at the time of the depression should perhaps be intoned each day by every thoughtful investor. 'I have always thought that if, even in the very presence of dizzily rising prices, we had all continuously repeated "two and two make four," much of the evil might have been averted. Similarly, even in the general moment of gloom in which this is written, when many begin to wonder if declines will never halt, the appropriate abracadabra may be "They always did".'

Keynes was one of the most sensible writers on the subject of investment. He said sagely that 'It is not sensible to pay 25 for an investment of which you believe the prospective yield to justify a value of 30, if you also believe that the market will value it at 20 at three months hence.'

We now apparently live in an era of People's Capitalism, when chatting about shares is supposedly almost as common as talking about the weather. One of the problems this has brought in its wake is the share bore, the person who knows it all. As an effective antidote, I suggest mastery of the following stock market terms. Full knowledge of these ought to see off the share bore in no time at all.

Bear: These depressing animals, who bet on shares falling, survive by spreading gloom and despondency and are a real turn-off at parties. They got their name because they were so lethargic most people assumed they were hibernating. Beware, though. Their hugs can be dangerous.

Bull: The opposite of bears. Bulls, believing shares will rise, are out-going, optimistic and cheerful pains-in-the-neck. They often sport wide lapels, slip-on shoes and golf umbrellas. So-called because the wild yarns they spin are usually reckoned to be complete fabrications.

Yield gap: This is the wide margin between the dividend a company declares, and the amount you receive after the taxman, accountant, wife, kids and postman have all had their share.

Tap stock: Whenever the government issues yet another gilt-edged stock, all the dealers race each other to the cold showers in order to revive themselves. The first to turn on the water wins, hence the nickname for this time-honoured ritual.

Jobber's turn: A fainting fit brought on by any criticism of their profession. Jobbers are particularly touchy about their ever-expanding 'spreads', usually brought on by too many City lunches. Incredibly shy, they tend to curl up in a ball and play dead at times of hectic market activity.

Market-maker: A contradiction in terms.

Insider dealing: If you act on a hot tip straight from the mouth of the nephew of the company's managing director's secretary's aunt's hairdresser, the authorities will slap the handcuffs on you sure as eggs, even though everybody else will escape Scot free. However, as there will be plenty of stockbrokers behind bars as well, transactions you make in prison will come under the header of Insider Dealing.

PE Ratio: This basic investment calculation (nothing to do with press-ups) is made vastly more useful by the fact that no two analysts ever produce the same figure. The best way to calculate a PE is to add the age of the company chairman to the number of employees. Divide that by the number you first thought of and you won't be far out.

Bed and Breakfast: This is a frequent hiding place for those trying to conceal their market profits from the taxman. Although the B&B is traditional, successful professionals these days prefer the comfort of five-star hotels.

I have railed in this book against the institutions, the Stock Exchange, government, stockbrokers and even, at the last, against private investors. We are none of us, however, perfect. I still recall with a shudder the time I was asked by a Northern stockbroking firm to speak at a gathering of about five hundred of their clients.

The week I was due to speak, I had to settle up for some shares I had bought through this broker. So I made especially sure that there were no mistakes with my cheque, that the date was correct, that I had put down the right year, that the words matched up perfectly with the figures and that I had spelled the broker's name correctly.

The day I was due to travel up to give my talk, a letter

arrived from the broker. Was it a good luck card? Last minute instructions on how to get there?

No. Enclosed was my cheque and a rather terse message: 'Dear Sir, A signature please!'

INDEX

Also by Simon Rose

FAIR SHARES
The layman's guide to buying and selling stocks and shares

Since the sale of British Telecom, the ranks of shareholders have been swelled through successive privatisation schemes and the growing number of employee share schemes. About a quarter of the adult population of the United Kingdom is now estimated to hold shares, and that figure looks set to increase with the government's new Personal Equity Plans. But the increase in numbers has not necessarily been accompanied by a higher level of understanding of how the stock market works.

If you are thinking of investing on the stock market, if you simply want to increase your understanding of how it works, or are perplexed by The Big Bang or PEPs, then *Fair Shares* is the ideal guide. A former stockbroker and now a leading financial journalist, Simon Rose is well placed to lead you through the mysteries of share dealing with this enlightening and thoroughly accessible introduction to the stock market.

'Never has the need for such a book been greater . . . An extremely useful and readable guide for investors considering going into the stock market.' *Financial Times*

'His dashing pace is hard to resist; by the time I had finished reading, I couldn't wait to get started.' *Punch*

ISBN: 1–85252–010–8
Price: £5.95